"Doctor Daniel has captured the essence of *The Mystery of Godliness* in this small volume. His background as an educator and a serious student of the Word over several decades has well prepared him to offer insights into this amazing topic that are both profound and yet simply stated. You will find this book both encouraging and challenging."
—*Robert Copley, Captain Colorado State Patrol (ret)*

"As a missionary to the poor, I'm always looking for Christian literature that will cut through the literary fog and present God in a real and interesting way. *The Mystery of Godliness* is a great read, down-to-earth, and straight to the heart. The fresh perspective may be the catalyst that brings a lost soul to the kingdom!"
—*Jack Dody from Equip International, author of* Abundaculture

"In the spring of 2018, I received a request from my brother, Dr. Daniel, to read a book that he had written. I had been teaching through Jerry Bridges' excellent work, *The Practice of Godliness*, in our adult Sunday School class at Emmanuel Chapel and so considered it very timely to read through his efforts. I was blessed and challenged with the presentation of sound biblical truths concerning this subject. Since I could recall a number of the events my brother referenced in his writing, it presented an even more down-to-earth application of this very heavy subject. Having pastored for 47 years and read many books on the subject of godliness, I do not lightly recommend any works on this subject. However, I am honored to give *The Mystery of Godliness* my endorsement and believe any serious student of the Word will be blessed by its study."
—*Pastor David Daniel, South Fork, CO*

"*The Mystery of Godliness* opens with the acknowledgment that godliness is a mystery, meaning it is a puzzle to be solved in partnership with the Holy Spirit, rooted in growing understanding of biblical truth, and lived out in the community of others seeking to live godly lives. Dr. Daniel delivers the goods, using the construct 'belief drives practice.' He provides personal, practical examples to explain his thinking and to make the principles behind 'belief drives practice' accessible for everyday application."

—*John Hopkins, Director of Communications, Every Nation Church, Seattle*

The Mystery of Godliness

What You Believe Is Important

Elden Daniel

RIVER BIRCH PRESS
Daphne, Alabama

The Mystery of Godliness
by Elden Daniel
Copyright ©2019, 2020 Elden Daniel

All rights reserved. This book is protected under the copyright laws of the United States of America. This book may not be copied or reprinted for commercial gain or profit.

Unless otherwise noted Scripture is taken from the King James Version of the Bible. In public domain.

Scripture marked NLT is taken from the Holy Bible, New Living Translation, copyright ©1996. Used by permission of Tyndale House Publishers, Inc., Wheaton IL 60189.

Scripture marked The Message is taken from *THE MESSAGE*. Copyright © by Eugene H. Peterson 1993, 1994, 1995, 1996, 2000, 2002. Used by permission of NavPress Publishing Group.

ISBN 978-1-951561-47-5 (Print)
ISBN 978-1-951561-48-2 (Ebook)
For Worldwide Distribution
Printed in the U.S.A.

River Birch Press
P.O. Box 868 • Daphne, AL 36526

Contents

Preface		v
1.	What Mysteries?	1
2.	What Is a Believer?	9
3.	The Believer's Role in the Mystery	17
4.	What Is Truth?	28
5.	Our Brain	33
6.	Belief Drives Practice	40
7.	Believers Applying Belief Drives Practice	52
8.	When People Believe Not-Truth	59
9.	Spiraling Down	73
10.	Truth and Life	84
11.	Transforming into Godliness	88
12.	Deeper Problems	105
13.	Finding Freedom	111
14.	Seeking Truth	123
15.	God's Economy	132
16.	What About Sin?	141
17.	Journey to Godliness	157
18.	What About Relationship?	173
19.	Who Are the Enemies?	178
20.	Cause and Effect	188
21.	Desire to Seek	192
Epilogue		197
References		200

Preface

I firmly believe that every believer has their own personal and mostly private journey toward godliness. We are each created uniquely different and travel our own private path through life. The Lord knows this and knows us. Since He is a personal Savior, each believer has a personal relationship with Him. It is a beautiful thing.

For bodily exercise profiteth little: but godliness is profitable unto all things, having promise of the life that now is, and of that which is to come. This is a faithful saying and worthy of all acceptation (I Timothy 4:8-9).

This book is about the journey and adventure for the believer to explore the mystery of godliness in route to becoming godly. Although the book is not about my personal journey, my personal journey does provide some perspective of what I write. How could it not? My progress in my personal journey can only be evaluated by the Lord Himself. I am too biased to be objective. In spite of the value of the verse, *"By their fruits you shall know them"* (Matthew 7:20), no one really knows me well enough to accurately evaluate. The same is true for you. *"For man looketh on the outward appearance, but the LORD looketh on the heart"* (I Samuel 16:7).

However, there are patterns and principles clearly revealed in the scriptures that give guidance into the mystery of godliness. In this book I seek to gather these patterns and principles and present them in a way that I believe may be helpful to you.

The intended audience for this book is the believer who has a committed desire to please the Lord and a hunger to know and love Him better. You will discover several themes in the book that I will mention here without giving away the gist of the story. I believe that every person, believer and unbeliever, is involved in a lifelong search for answers to these two questions: Who am I? and How does the world work? I believe that everyone's journey in life involves learning and that learning changes that person.

I believe in the accuracy and universal application of the principle: Beliefs drive practice. You will find that the book includes the quoting of many scriptures. Since the word of God is truth, how could I not include many scriptures? If these themes seem mysterious and capture your interest and curiosity, you are ready to read the book.

I can relate to what J. I. Packer said in the closing sentence of his forward in *Knowing God*: "and if what is written here helps anyone in the way the meditations behind the writing has helped me, the work will have been abundantly worth while" (p. 7).

Chapter 1

What Mysteries?

"Mystery" means in the language of the New Testament, something that had long remained hidden but then came to be known for the first time." Dallas Willard (*Divine Conspiracy*)

Mysteries are intriguing and stimulate curiosity. Mysteries challenge us to seek a solution. When watching or reading a mystery, we often try to discover the solution as the story unfolds before it is revealed at the end. Often when reading or viewing a mystery, we as readers or viewers are given insight into the mystery by the author that the characters do not have. There is even a popular board game called Clue where players try to solve a mystery.

Clues are a key to solving a mystery. First we have to look for clues, then we have to recognize the clues, and finally we need to figure out how the clues relate to the solution. Sometimes there are clues within clues. Discovering a clue is rewarding and motivation for looking for the next one.

We are going to be looking at clues that will help discover the mystery of godliness. We will also discover how the clues relate to each other in finding solutions. Since you have selected this book and already read this far, I am assuming that you have a personal desire to become godly.

Let me encourage you that you are about to embark on a journey that will use clues to guide you into understanding the mystery of godliness and assist you in your quest for a godly life. Since you know the Lord Jesus and love and admire Him, don't you want to be like Him?

As I read about the mysteries in the scripture, I get the sense that the scriptures are revealing information about them that believers do not get. In the New Testament, we find that there are many mysteries. Let's look at some of them by category and end by focusing on the mystery of godliness. Then we will travel through the rest of this book, examining many clues as to the mystery of godliness.

The mysteries of the kingdom of heaven:

*And the disciples came, and said unto him, Why speakest thou unto them in parables? He answered and said unto them, Because it is given unto you to know the **mysteries** of the kingdom of heaven, but to them it is not given* (Matthew 13:10-11*)*.

The mysteries of the kingdom of God:

*And his disciples asked him, saying, What might this parable mean? And he said, Unto you it is given to know the **mysteries** of the kingdom of God: but to others in parables; that seeing they might not see, and hearing they might not understand* (Luke 8:9-10).

The mysteries of the wisdom of God:

*But we speak the wisdom of God in a **mystery**, even the hidden wisdom, which God ordained before the world unto glory: Which none of the princes of this world knew: for had they known it, they would not have crucified the Lord of glory* (I Corinthians 2:7-8).

What Mysteries?

The mysteries of God:

*Let a man so account of us, as of the ministers of Christ, and stewards of the **mysteries** of God* (I Corinthians 4:1).

*That their hearts might be comforted, being knit together in love, and unto all riches of the full assurance and understanding, to the acknowledgement of the **mystery** of God, and of the Father, and of Christ; In whom are hid all treasures of wisdom and knowledge* (Colossians 2:2-3).

The revelation of the mystery:

*Now to him is of power to stablish you according to my gospel, and the preaching of Jesus Christ, according to the revelation of the **mystery**, which was kept since the world began* (Romans 16:25).

The mystery of rapture:

*Behold I shew you a **mystery**: We shall not all sleep, but we shall all be changed, In a moment, in the twinkling of an eye, at the last trump: for the trumpet shall sound, and the dead shall be raised incorruptible, and we shall be changed. For this corruptible must put on incorruption, and this mortal shall put on immortality* (I Corinthians 15:51-53).

The mystery of His will:

*Having been made known unto us the **mystery** of his will according to the good pleasure which he hath purposed himself: That in the dispensation of the fullness of times he might gather together in one all things in Christ, both which are in heaven, and which are in the earth; even in him* (Ephesians 1:9-10).

The mystery of Christ:

*How that by revelation he made known unto me the **mystery**;*

*(as I wrote afore in few words, Whereby when ye read, ye may understand my knowledge in the **mystery** of Christ) which in other ages was not made known unto the sons of men, as it is now revealed unto the holy apostles and prophets by the Spirit* (Ephesians 3:3-5).

*Withal praying also for us, and God would open unto us a door of utterance, to speak the **mystery** of Christ, for which I am also in bonds* (Colossians 4:3).

The mystery of Christ as Creator:

*And to make all men see what is the fellowship of the **mystery** which from the beginning of the world hath been hid in God, who created all things by Christ Jesus* (Ephesians 3:9).

The mystery of the gospel:

*And for me, that utterance may be given unto me, that I may open my mouth boldly, to make known the **mystery** of the gospel* (Ephesians 6:19).

The mystery of Christ in you the hope of glory:

*Whereof I am made a minister, according to the dispensation of God which is given to me for you, to fulfil the word of God. Even the **mystery** which hath been hid from ages and from generations, but now is made manifest in the saints: To whom God would make known what is the riches of the glory of this **mystery** among the Gentiles; which is Christ in you, the hope of glory* (Colossians 1:25-27).

The mystery of faith:

*Holding the **mystery** of the faith in a pure conscience* (I Timothy 3:9).

The mystery of iniquity:

*For the **mystery** of iniquity doth already work: only he who*

What Mysteries?

now letteth will let, until he be taken out of the way (II Thessalonians 2:7).

The mystery of godliness:

*And without controversy great is the **mystery** of godliness: God was manifest in the flesh, justified in the Spirit, seen of angels, preached unto Gentiles, believed on in the world, received up into glory* (I Timothy 3:16).

Let's pause and think about the concept of godliness. Simply put, the word "godliness" would imply being like God. If we observe someone whom we would say exhibits friendliness, we understand that person is acting like a friend. If we say that some people are demonstrating neighborliness, we understand that they are behaving in a good, neighborly manner. Therefore, godliness must mean to be acting like God acts.

J. I. Packer defined godliness as: "Godliness means responding to God's revelation in trust and obedience, faith and worship, faith and praise, submission and service. Life must be seen and lived in the light of God's Word. This, and nothing else, is true religion" (*Knowing God* p. 16).

Clearly, this does not mean that we somehow possess the attributes of God. However, the many behaviors listed in the fruit of the Spirit along with the frequent directions on how a believer should act indicate expectation for believers. *"But the fruit of the Spirit is love, joy, peace, longsuffering, gentleness, goodness, faith, Meekness, temperance: against such there is no law"* (Galatians 5:22-23). Therefore, godliness must mean a person acts with godly behavior.

But how does this happen? How does a believer come to act in a godly manner? What are the clues? That is the mystery! We may not be able to completely solve that mystery, but we can come to understand much about how it works. That will be our journey and goal!

Beyond and Other

With that introduction, let's look more closely at the concept of mystery and godliness. When it comes to knowing and understanding God, there is that which we can know that has been revealed by God in His Word and that which has been learned experientially, but there is that which is *"beyond"* or *"other."* Let's concede that there is more to and about God than we could possibly know. This is not a problem. It is just a fact. God is greater than we are or than we can ever be. This is a comfort because we belong to and serve One who is greater than we are.

Eugene Peterson summarizes:

> God is more than can be comprehended. "A God that can be understood is no God." We cannot "know" God in a way that explains everything about him. The only way that we can approach God is through worship: holy, holy, holy. (*Christ Plays in Ten Thousand Places* p. 306)

Let's pause to think about the *"otherness"* or the *"beyondness"* of God. His attributes set Him apart from His creation. We know some things, but He knows everything. We have some power, but He has all power. We can be in a place, but He is everywhere. We had a beginning, but He has always been and will always be. His knowledge, power, and existence is beyond ours. It seems only logical to concede that there is more than we can experience. Some examples: The Holy Spirit prays in words that cannot be uttered: *"beyond"* and *"other."*

Eugene Peterson in his book, *Christ Plays in Ten Thousand Places*, describes this beautifully:

What Mysteries?

There is a lot going on in us and this world, far exceeding what we are capable of taking in. In dealing with God, we are dealing in mystery, in what we know, what we cannot control or deal with on our terms. We need to know this, for we live in a world that over-respects the practical. We want God to be "relevant" to our lifestyle. We want what we can, as we say, "get a handle on." There is immense peer pressure to reduce God to fit immediate needs and expectations. But God is never a commodity to use. In a functionalized world in which we are all trained to understand ourselves in terms of what we can do, we are faced with a reality that we cannot control. And so, we cultivate reverence. We are in the presence of One who is both before and beyond us. We listen and wait. Presumption—God-on-demand on our terms—is exposed as simply silly. Defining God down to the level of our emotions, and thinking and demanding that God work by terms of our agenda, is set aside in favor of a life of worship and prayer, obedience and love—a way of life open and responsive to what God is doing rather than one in which we plot strategies to get God involved in what we are doing. Trinity keeps pulling us into a far larger world than we can imagine on our own (p. 46).

Paul in his vision in the third heaven saw things that could not be uttered: *"beyond"* and *"other."* A.W. Tozer in the book, *Knowledge of the Holy,* says:

> Every man lives by faith, the nonbeliever as well as the saint; the one by faith in natural laws and the other by the faith in God. Every man throughout his entire life constantly accepts without understanding. The most learned sage can be reduced to silence with one simple question, *"What?"* The answer to that question lies forever in the abyss of unknowing beyond any man's ability to discover. "God understandeth the way thereof, and he knoweth the place thereof," but mortal man never (p. 25).

One of the concepts we gather from the scriptures is: there is that which some have called the economy of God. There are principles and laws that work in God's economy. The principles' origin is God Himself and He has revealed some of them.

An example is that all mankind can be placed in one of two categories: those who are believers and are saved, and those who are unbelievers and are lost. *"No man comes to the Father but by Me"* (John 14:6). *"There is none other name under heaven given among men, whereby which we must be saved"* (Acts 4:12). Clearly there are behaviors that are good and righteous, and there are behaviors that are bad and evil.

There is a way that things work in God's economy, and there is a way that the mystery of godliness works. In the next chapter, we will be exploring the basics by looking at a foundational clue.

Chapter 2

What Is a Believer?

Lost

Many years ago, my wife and I were elk hunting with my parents. The weather conditions were very challenging. It was snowing very hard, big wet flakes; the snow was piling up very quickly and approaching a foot deep. My wife and I were out in the woods on a "walk-about" in spite of the conditions.

The conventional wisdom is not to be out in the woods in heavy weather. The visibility was not good. I had hunted in this area of the mountain for years and was very confident in my knowledge of them. My wife, however, was not familiar and was dependent on me. One good thing was the fact that it was not terribly cold.

I became a little concerned about where we were because some of the surroundings did not look familiar for where I thought we were. Then we begin to hear a lot of honking from a vehicle. I can remember that we commented that someone must be lost and kind of chuckled. The honking continued and our chuckling changed to concern for whoever was lost. Then we heard a vehicle driving and soon saw a pickup with another hunter.

I began to become a little more concerned because I had just seen a fence that I didn't recognize, and I couldn't place the road that the pickup had been using. I had been using a certain mountain as a point of reference for direction because we wanted to get back to where we had started that morning. The snow was so heavy, though, that my mountain of reference kept disappearing and reappearing. All this time we keep hearing the honking.

After the pickup sighting, I realized that the mountain I had been using for reference was not the mountain that I thought it was. Fortunately, I was able to reorient myself and locate the proper mountain to provide appropriate orientation. Needless to say, we changed the direction of our hike. It turns out that the guy in the pickup met up with my dad and mom and told them where he had seen us. This helped my parents to start driving toward where they thought we were.

Happily, we met up and they saved us a long walk. The point of the story is this: It was my parents who were doing the honking to help guide us back, and those who were lost were my wife and me. A person can be lost and not know it, and another person can be following a person who is lost and not know that they are lost too.

The honking was a call to be saved. It is not unusual for skiers, hunters, or hikers to become lost in snowstorms and their bodies not found and recovered until the next summer after the snow melts. Those lost are in danger and need to be saved whether they know it or not.

The invitation to be saved is offered to lost sinners. Sinners are in danger. A person has to first recognize that they are lost sinners before coming to Christ. The scriptures help us in the understanding of sin. *"He that knoweth to do good and doeth it not, to him it is sin"* (James 4:17). *"Whatsoever is not of faith is sin"* (Romans 14:23). *"...by the law is knowledge of sin"* (Romans 3:20). Here is an interesting twist. You may ask, "But what about those who do not know or have access to the law of God?" The answer:

For when the Gentiles which have not the law, do by nature the things contained in the law, these, having not the law, are a law unto themselves. Which show the work of the law written in their hearts, their conscience also bearing witness, and their thoughts the mean while accusing or else excusing one another (Romans 2:14-15*)*.

There is a law that is written on everyone's heart. This law is the knowledge of right and wrong. One of the tests for insanity in court cases is: Did the defendant know right from wrong? We will be exploring this concept much deeper as we move along.

Saved

Here we have a fundamental clue. A person has to become saved and be a believer in the Lord Jesus and His saving work on the cross for there to be a possibility of becoming godly. This is so basic and perhaps so obvious, but a strong foundation is critical to understanding. The story is told that the famous football coach, Vince Lombardi, would begin each training camp holding a football and making the statement, "Gentlemen, this is a football." Basics are important.

To keep in context of our quest for solving the mystery of godliness, let's look at another clue and perhaps the most important one: believers are transformed.

And be not conformed to this world: but be ye transformed by the renewing of your mind, that ye may prove what is that good, and acceptable, and perfect, will of God (Romans 12:2).

A change occurs that is demonstrated by becoming a nonconformist to this world. Because the mind is renewed, behaviors and actions occur that result in conforming to the good, acceptable, and perfect will of God. It is helpful to notice that process is indicated by the choice of the word, *"renewing."* The "ing" implies an ongoing process.

What makes this transformation possible? What are the necessary conditions? Let's explore them. As indicated earlier, the first and basic condition to be satisfied is a person must be a believer. There are several phrases used to define a believer. We say that a believer is a person who has been saved. The question is, saved from what? The answer is, saved from the just judgment for sins.

We can think of the opposite of saved as lost and often refer to those who are not saved as lost. It seems logical that a person must first understand that they are lost before they seek to be saved. The scripture says that, *"For all have sinned, and come short of the glory of God"* (Romans 3:23). We know it is possible for a person to be lost and not know it.

The question for believers is believe in what? The answer is to believe in Jesus Christ and His atoning work on the cross. Everyone has a belief system, and everyone functions daily based on it. Belief is determined by decisions and choices. If I believe it is cold outside, I will decide not to go out without a coat. If I believe it is important and proper to be polite to people, I will make an effort to be polite. If I believe it is wrong to steal, I will choose to not steal. The demonstration of that belief occurs when I have an opportunity to steal something and I choose not to steal.

Belief takes place in our minds. Our behaviors and actions are based on those beliefs. Looking back to the transforming that takes place in the life of a believer, remember the phrase, *"renewing of the mind."*

What Is a Believer?

Born Again

Another phrase that is often used is born again believer. This concept comes from John 3:3 when Nicodemus was told by Jesus, *"Verily, verily, I say unto thee, Except a man be born again, he cannot see the kingdom of God."* Nicodemus naturally was puzzled by this response and mentions the impossibility of entering again into his mother's womb. Jesus explains:

> *Verily, verily, I say unto thee, Except a man be born of the water and of the Spirit, he cannot enter into the Kingdom of God. That which is born of flesh is flesh; and that which is born of Spirit is spirit. Marvel not that I said unto thee, Ye must be born again. The wind bloweth where it listeth, and thou hearest the sound thereof, but canst not tell whence it cometh, and whither it goeth: so is every one that is born of the Spirit* (John 3: 5-8).

We can summarize that a born-again believer, and technically that is the only kind of true believer there is, is someone who has been born again spiritually. Notice by the use of the wind analogy something that is invisible and yet very real is used to describe the mystery of the spiritual rebirth. Once again, a concept that is *"other"* and *"beyond."*

Saint

There are other words to identify believers in scripture. For example: the word "saint" is used sometimes in scripture. Now because of the practice of Catholics to identify what they consider outstanding, deceased Catholics that meet certain qualifications as saints, some may feel uncomfortable with considering themselves saints. In humbleness we tend to think of ourselves as rather ordinary believers rather than special.

Want proof? *"Paul, an apostle of Jesus Christ by the will of God,* to the saints which are at Ephesus, and to the faithful in Christ Jesus" (Ephesians 1:1). "To the saints and faithful brethren in Christ which are at Colosse: Grace be unto you, and peace, from God our Father and the Lord Jesus Christ" (Colossians 1:2). That being said from the truth of scripture, believers are saints. Peter and John even identify believers as priests and kings.

> But ye are a chosen generation, a royal priesthood, an holy nation, a peculiar people; that ye should shew forth the praises of him who hath called you out of darkness into his marvelous light (I Peter 2:9).

> And hath made us kings and priests unto God and his Father; to him be glory and dominion for ever and ever. Amen (Revelation 1:6).

Holy

The journey to godliness also involves believers becoming holy and pure. We might feel presumption to think of ourselves as holy or pure. We may think that such thinking is prideful or self-righteous. Our awareness of our own sins keeps clouding our image of ourselves as being either holy or pure, but the scripture is clear.

> But as he which hath called you is holy, so be ye holy in all manner of conversation; Because it is written, Be ye holy; for I am holy (I Peter 1:15-16).

> Follow peace with all men, and holiness, without which no man shall see the Lord (Hebrews 12:14).

> Let no man despise thy youth; but be thou an example of the believers, in word, in conversation, in charity, in spirit, in faith, in purity." Remember that the transformation and "renewing of the mind" is a progressive process. Ultimately, when we go to be with the Lord we will be holy and pure (I Timothy 4:12).

What Is a Believer?

That he might present it to himself a glorious church, not having spot, or wrinkle, or any such thing; but that it should be holy and without blemish (Ephesians 5:27).

Let's take a closer look at the value of the invisible:

While we look not at the things which are seen, but at the things which are not seen: for the things which are seen are temporal; but the things which are not seen are eternal (II Corinthians 4:18).

One of the clearest explanations of the process of how someone becomes a believer is found in Romans 10:9-10.

That if thou shalt confess with thy mouth the Lord Jesus, and shalt believe in thy heart that God than raised Him from the dead, thou shalt be saved. For with the heart man believeth unto righteousness; and with the mouth confession is made unto salvation.

There is heart belief and visible and audible profession. The heart belief drives the practice of confession.

Indwelling Holy Spirit

What happens in this very essential rebirth? What changes occur? This is mysterious! Notice that Jesus stated that the new birth involved an action by the Spirit. He is referring to the Holy Spirit. From scripture we learn a marvelous truth has happened when a person is saved, becomes a believer, and is born again: they become indwelt with the Holy Spirit. The Spirit of God actually comes to reside in the believer.

The indwelling of the Holy Spirit is a critical understanding in exploring the mystery of godliness. This reality is repeatedly taught in the New Testament. This is a fabulous truth to try to grasp, that the Holy Spirit is actually residing in the body of a believer. Where in the body? Often, we think of the Holy Spirit being in the believer's heart. We say things like, "I have Jesus or the Holy Spirit in my heart." But sometimes we refer to the Holy Spirit being in a person's soul or in a person's mind. In trying to locate the position of the Holy Spirit, we are actually determining that the Holy Spirit dwells in the core or essence of a person.

Remember the Holy Spirit is invisible like the wind so we can't x-ray or CAT scan to find Him. A. W. Tozer says, "…man is a creature having a spirit and declares that he is a spirit having a body." We tend to think of ourselves with a body that contains a spirit; while actually, from God's perspective, we are a spirit that is in a body. Very different view!

Scripture clearly teaches that the Holy Spirit will never leave a believer. Believers are sealed by the Holy Spirit (Ephesians 1:13). Jesus described the Holy Spirit as a Comforter (John 14:16). The Holy Spirit teaches and guides a believer (John 14:26). The Holy Spirit gives revelation to believers and convicts believers of sin (John 16: 8-11).

As mentioned earlier, the Holy Spirit prays for us in words that cannot be uttered (Romans 8:26). I picture this as a process of interpretation in which my prayers to God are interpreted into the unutterable words and presented to the Godhead. This is another example of *"other"* and *"beyond."*

The decision to come to Christ for salvation results in not only the forgiveness of sins and escape from judgment but the supernatural insertion of the Holy Spirit which provides the capacity for godliness. (John 14:17) The mystery is not solved, but it is more and more understandable. The process for the individual believer to become godly is a work of God in that individual. It is also clearly not a passive thing for the believer because each person has a role in the process of becoming more godly.

Chapter 3

The Believer's Role in the Mystery

More Like Jesus Would I Be

More like Jesus would I be,
Let my Savior dwell in me;
Fill my soul with peace and love,
Make me gentle as a dove;
More like Jesus while I go,
Pilgrim in the world below;
Poor in Spirit would I be;
Let my Savior dwell in me.

What is the role of the individual believer in the transformation into godliness? Enter the element of the individual's will. Hebrews 11:6 says, *"But without faith it is impossible to please Him: for he that cometh to God must believe that that He is, and that He is the rewarder of them that diligently seek Him."* Here is found a foundational principle. A person must "will" to diligently seek God founded on the principle that first He exists (He is) and followed with the understanding that this seeking will be rewarded by God.

We can infer that initially this means that seeking Him will result in the reward of finding Him. God has revealed Himself as the great "I am." God revealed Himself to Moses that way, and Christ revealed Himself to His captors in the Garden that way. Eugene Peterson lists Christ's revelation of Himself as "I am."

> Seven times Jesus uses the "I am/egoeimi" formula with a predicate, a metaphor that serves as a parable that fills in details of who He is and what He is up to: the bread of life (John 6:35), the light of the world (8:12), the gate for the sheep (10:7), the good shepherd (10:14), the resurrection and the life (11:25), the way, the truth, and the life (14:6), the true vine (15:1) (*Christ Plays in Ten Thousand Places* p. 90).

In other places in Scripture, we read that the fear of God is the beginning of wisdom. Essentially, the path to godliness is through belief in what God says is true. Remember that in John 14:6, Christ stated that He was, *"The way, the truth and the life."* As we seek to unravel the mystery of godliness, we have established the salvation essentials that result in a person becoming a believer who has the indwelling Holy Spirit.

We can now see that faith (belief) is linked both to the individual's will and to truth. We will be looking more closely at how critical the concept of truth is to understanding the mystery of godliness, but first let's look at some other connections that believers enjoy with God.

What to do with the will? The scriptures indicate that the believer's will is to be yielded to God. Romans 6:13 says,

> *Neither yield ye your members as instruments of unrighteousness unto sin: but yield yourselves unto God, as those that are alive from the dead, and your members as instruments of righteousness unto God.*

Jesus set the example while He was walking on earth as a man. He repeatedly demonstrated that He had yielded His will to the will of His Father. Jesus was a model of a yielded walk with God. John 8:29 says, *".... for I do always those things that please him"* In the garden as He was facing the specter of the cross, He asked if it

The Believer's Role in the Mystery

would be possible for this cup to pass from Him but stated to the Father, *"...not what I will but, what thou wilt"* (Mark 14:36).

The faithful believers surrender their will to the will of God. This decision is based on trust in God. This should be easy, but the heart of the believer needs the transforming experience to move into that relationship of trust. Let's look at what Eugene Peterson has to say:

> The often disregarded scriptural rule is that we cannot be *made* to believe. Belief by its very nature requires assent and participation, trust and commitment. When we believe we are at our most personal and intimate with another, with the Other. Belief cannot be forced. If we are bullied or seduced or manipulated to believe, we do not end up believing, we end up intimidated or raped or used. And we are less not more (*Christ Plays in Ten Thousand Places* p. 94).

We often conceptualize this progression as spiritual growth and think of it as a maturing process for the individual. Scripture clearly refers to those who are babes in Christ and believers are exhorted to grow up in Christ. The transformation is a progression that includes a *"renewing of the mind."* The believers change into the image of Christ and this is part of the mystery of godliness.

See then that ye walk circumspectly, not as fools, but as wise (Ephesians 5:15).

My Body

Let's add to the question: Who am I? the question: How do I work? It is important to have understanding about how our physical body functions. We will be particularly interested in how our brain functions because this is how we will be processing both **not-truth** and the **truth**. The believer's body is called a temple.

Know ye not that ye are the temple of God, and that the Holy Spirit of God dwelleth in you? (I Corinthians 3:16)

What? Know ye not that your body is the temple of the Holy Ghost which is in you, which ye have of God, and ye are not your own? (I Corinthians 6:19).

The temples of our bodies are cited as temporary. Our bodies are passing away. They are deteriorating. Dust to dust! We often hear this read at funerals.

For this corruptible must put on incorruption, and this mortal must put on immortality. So when this corruptible shall have put on incorruption, and this mortal shall have put on immortality, then shall be brought to pass the saying that is written, Death is swallowed up in victory (I Corinthians 15:53-54).

What about our bodies? God has created unique individual bodies. DNA is currently used to identify the uniqueness of specific individuals. Through scientific research and the medical field, we have come to know much about our bodies. Systems are categorized: digestive, nervous, circulatory, respiratory, reproductive, muscular, skeletal, etc. Different parts are labeled and functions are described. The brain has been extensively studied.

It seems that new insights into these systems are being discovered all the time. The structure and function of our bodies is truly amazing. The body's capacity to grow and heal itself is fascinating. The process of conception and fetal development exceeds the imagination. God's wonder in the creation of our bodies is to be proclaimed. However, as wonderful as all of this is, these bodies are still only temporary.

As discussed earlier, our spirit, the real us that is eternal and where the Holy Spirit abides for the believer is only housed (the temple) for a short period of time: conception to physical death. But even

The Believer's Role in the Mystery

though the body is temporary and we are more than our bodies, while in these bodies our transformation to godliness occurs.

We come back to Romans 6:13,

> *Neither yield ye your members as instruments of unrighteousness unto sin: but yield yourselves unto God, as those that are alive from the dead, and your members as instruments of righteousness unto God.*

God uses our physical brains to process His information and to operate in a relationship with Him. Hence our minds are being renewed. We use our speech capacity and hearing ability to communicate with others about God's revelation. We use our seeing capacity to read His Word. We use our strength and limbs to serve others for believers are to yield their bodies to Christ. Romans 12:1 states,

> *I beseech you therefore, brethren, by the mercies of God, that ye present your bodies a living sacrifice, holy, acceptable unto God, which is your reasonable service.*

You see, our route to godliness at this time is played out in these temporary bodies. This includes all the amazing features and capacities as well as the limitations. Eugene Peterson makes it clear in *Christ Plays in Ten Thousand Places*:

> These bodies of ours with their five senses are not impediments to a life of faith; our sensuality is not a barrier to spirituality; it is our only access to it. Thomas Aquinas was convinced that *asensuality* was a vice, the rejection of one's senses too often leading to sacrilege. When St. John wanted to assure some early believers of the authenticity of his spiritual experience, he did it by calling on the witness of his senses of sight, hearing and touch—"what we have heard...seen with our eyes...touched with our hands, concerning the word of life" (I John 13). In the opening sentence

of 1 John he calls on the witness of his senses seven times (p. 198).

Ultimately, when we leave these bodies and are changed, we don't know how our sensing and reasoning capacity will function. The new body is another mystery. We will come back and look more closely at ways the body participates in the mystery of godliness.

Belonging

Let's look at some elements of belonging. We will see some frameworks of relationship that God uses to explain our connection to God as believers. It feels good to belong, and sometimes it is a painful feeling to be excluded when we want to belong. We understand how nice it is to be an insider in a desirable group and how it hurts to be on the outside.

All kinds of social tension and strife surround issues of inclusion and exclusion. To be included is to belong. We use symbols to show our identification with belonging to a group. I have caps that I wear that identify me with my favorite football and baseball teams. I have other hats that identify organizations I belong to and support. I have decals on my vehicle windows that proclaim that I belong to an organization.

Uniforms show belonging. Many subcultures have specific attire that indicates their affiliation. Think of some: bikers, runners, cowboys and cowgirls, bicyclists, etc. Gang members have signs and colors. Sports teams, professions, and military branches have uniforms that identify belonging. Flags and pennants are flown to declare allegiance. Belonging is a big deal!

Scripture declares that believers are citizens of the Kingdom of God. There is the earthly Kingdom of God that a person becomes a member of upon accepting Christ as Savior. When a person is born

The Believer's Role in the Mystery

again, they are born into the Kingdom of God. There is also a heavenly Kingdom of God of which believers are also members. Don't be confused—these are the same kingdoms. Kingdoms have kings. The Lord Jesus is the King.

Remember the sign on the cross that read, King of the Jews. Kingdoms have subjects and believers are the subjects. Historically, many kingdoms have despots but not in this kingdom. God's kingdom is a kingdom of love. Kingdoms have rules, customs, and practices. In the Kingdom of God, the behavioral standard is godliness. The believer is transformed into a new person with a new mind who behaves appropriately in the kingdom. This is not a burdensome thing.

Since it is a kingdom of love, the motivator is love, specifically the believer's love for the Lord Jesus. John 14:15 says, *"If you love me, keep my commandments."* It is a really good thing to belong in the Kingdom of God. As understanding grows about what it means to be a member of the Kingdom of God, it feels really good!

It is time for a reminder. Let's go back to the beginning and review a couple of verses about mysteries.

> *And the disciples came, and said unto him, Why speakest thou unto them in parables? He answered and said unto them, Because it is given unto you to know the **mysteries** of the kingdom of heaven, but to them it is not given* (Matthew 13:10-11).

The mysteries of the Kingdom of God:

> *And his disciples asked him, saying, What might this parable mean? And he said, Unto you it is given to know the **mysteries** of the kingdom of God: but to others in parables; that seeing they might not see, and hearing they might not understand* (Luke 8:9-10).

Believers are also part of the family of God, sons and daughters. We all have earthly families. Many and perhaps most of the families are a place of acceptance and nurture. The experience is usually overall a good one. However, in some cases for some people, the family experience is not good at all. Even the best of family experiences will have some elements that are not so good.

Earthly families are made up of sinners. Biological family links are not made by choice. People are born into the family they are born into, period. Being part of the family of God shows connectedness and closeness. All members of the family of God have God as their Father. That relationship brings with it the care, support, and protection that a father gives to his children. In God's family the standard is love. My wife and I have received an inheritance from our parents and plan to leave an inheritance to our children. As members of the family of God, we have an inheritance. I Peter 1:4 states, *"To an inheritance incorruptible, and undefiled, and that fadeth not away, reserved in heaven for you."*

Sheep Need a Shepherd

Scripture gives us other models of connectedness and belonging to God for believers. In John 10, believers are identified as sheep with Christ as the good shepherd who gives His life for the sheep. As a shepherd, Christ leads the sheep and the sheep know His voice. My wife and I have a small band of sheep. What we have learned while caring for the sheep makes John 10 very real to us.

We have discovered that most of our sheep are rather calm around us, but when a stranger comes along, the sheep immediately become agitated and alert. This is not because the strangers are doing anything wrong, but because they are just interested in seeing the sheep. But they are strangers and the sheep do not know them! We have learned to be careful to not act like a predator, and we also

The Believer's Role in the Mystery

learned the value of talking to the sheep. There is every indication that the sheep hear our voice and recognize it.

We have also learned that often we can more effectively lead the sheep than drive them. For example, each year we wean the lambs from their mothers when they are about three months old. One time right after weaning, the lambs were confused about going out to pasture. There were no adult sheep to lead them out as they were accustomed. The lambs seemed stuck. Rather than trying to drive them out to pasture, I just walked out ahead of them and led them to the pasture. Like good little sheep, they just fell into line and followed me out. Problem solved!

We have the practice of bringing the sheep in from the pasture and shutting them up in their pen (the equivalent of a fold) every night to protect them from marauding predators. Almost always the sheep come into the corral on their own, and we only have to shut them up in the corral. One of our pastures has a dividing fence and the open end of the fence where the sheep can freely cross through can act like a bottleneck. Two different times in different years and with different sets of lambs, the lambs failed to come into the corral in the evening. It was necessary to go get them to bring them into the corral.

Here is the scene. It is after dark. I was able to drive my pickup down the road near the bottleneck. This is where the lambs seemed to be stuck. I shined the pickup headlights out into the field so I could see the lambs. The lambs seemed concerned and confused. I attempted to get behind them and drive them through the opening but to no avail. It didn't work. Then I remembered to try to lead them. All I had to do was get in front of them and call out to them, and as I moved through the opening and toward the corral, they very calmly fell in line and followed me all the way to the corral.

Another example of the sheep hearing the shepherd's voice was told to me by a friend who is a believer. Jim and his wife, Jan, were visiting their daughter, Julie, who was working in Kuwait. Jim related how the flocks of sheep would come in from the pasture at evening, and he noticed that the sheep had been painted with different colors of spray paint.

Then an interesting thing happened. Different people would call out some words or sounds. When they did, the sheep that had the same color paint would fall out into a smaller flock and go with their owners. The sheep knew their shepherd's voice and followed. Believers have a Shepherd, and we are to hear His voice and follow and we follow because we are His sheep. The Lord's sheep! I like to think that it implies a submissive spirit toward the Lord.

> *To him the porter openeth; and the sheep hear his voice: and he calleth his own sheep by name, and leadeth them out. And when he putteth forth his own sheep, he goeth before them, and the sheep follow him: for they know his voice* (John 10:3-4).

Another metaphor describing our relationship with the Lord is that Christ is the Vine and believers are the branches. The branches draw their life from the vine. Sometimes the branches need to be pruned to bear more fruit. This too is part of the mystery of godliness. In addition, the church is identified as the body of Christ, and individuals are parts of that body.

Looking more closely at all of these models of belonging, we notice that although each has a wonderful, personal, and individual application, there is also a feature that includes others.

We belong to God and we also belong to other believers. The Kingdom of God has many citizens. The family of God has many children. We call each other brother and sister. The sheep are in a flock. The vine has many branches. The body has many members. These others include believers that are currently alive and those from throughout the ages. The present belonging is really part of a greater belonging. This is a good thing!

Chapter 4

What Is Truth?

Fredrick Douglas said, "There was no such thing as new truth. Error might be old or new, but truth was as old as the universe."

We began our exploration about the mystery of godliness by identifying the initial necessity of becoming a believer by being born again. We discovered that the regeneration experience of becoming a believer included the indwelling of the Holy Spirit, which provides the capacity to enable a person to become godly. We also looked at the importance of the believer yielding their will to the will of God.

Then we examined several models that demonstrate our relationship of belonging to God as well as the company of other believers. We inquired into how our temporary earthly bodies figure into the mystery of godliness. Jesus said in John 14 that He was *"the way, the truth and the life."* Now we look more closely at how the truth is involved in the mystery of godliness and how this happens in our temporary earthly bodies. In our quest to diligently seek Him and our desire to become godly, let's plunge into more detail.

Truth! What is truth? Jesus said that He is the truth (John 14). Pilate asked what is truth? Then after saying that he found no fault

What Is Truth?

in this Man, he said take Him and kill him. Total contradiction! In our search for clues we must state the obvious, a clue must be true or it is of no value and should be discarded.

Let's think of two categories—**Truth** and **Not-Truth**—In your mind think of two columns; one with the label **truth** and one with the label **not-truth** or perhaps visualize a decision tree—you know the kind you might set up to reach a decision about buying a new car. One side is the pros and the other side is the cons. However, in this case one side is **truth** and the other is **not-truth**.

Now under **truth** you would only have the word truth because anything less than the truth would have to go into the **not-truth** column. All half or partial truths would go into the **not-truth** column because the **truth** is pure. Remember the oath used in court, "Do you swear to tell the whole truth and nothing but the truth." Also, most lies have some element or appearance of some truth to provide enough credibility to deceive. The truth we are talking about is God's truth (thought, word, and deed).

Under the **not-truth** column, there are many words we can list: lie, white lie, half-truth, deception, fabrication, prevarication, exaggeration, discounting, false perceptions, wrong conclusions, inaccuracies, disinformation, fake news. Major Ian Thomas says, "Every lie is about the truth."

What I am doing with this concept of the **truth** and **not-truth** is creating what is called a construct. A construct is an idea, concept, proposition, or principle. I like the word construct because a construct is made of related elements that fit together—hence construct as in constructions.

Also, I will be introducing additional constructs that through a process called scaffolding will come together to support each other. Another reason for liking the term construct is that it goes so well with scaffolding. We want all our constructs to be true. I assert that the construct of **truth** and **not-truth** is a universal truth.

The **truth** exists independently of our believing or accepting it as **truth**. The **truth** does not become **truth** just because we decide to categorize it as **truth**. This is a good thing because we do not have to create it. We simply have to identify or discern **truth**.

Self-System

Now let's work on another construct. During this time in our existence, we have a body, an earthly body. In 1953 Harry Stack Sullivan came up with the concept called self-system. If you Google him, you will see a whole lot of psychobabble. We are not interested in that. I want to focus on two elements of the self-system—self-awareness and making sense of the world. This is a developmental process.

First, let's look at self-awareness. Think about a baby and how we marvel as they seem to discover their hands and feet. Eventually, they begin to talk and we hear words like "no!" or "mine!" These are clues that they are on the road to becoming aware of themselves as an individual.

The point is we all figure out that we are a unique individual, and through contacts with relatives and in communication with others, we learn there is that part that is only me. Closely associated is an awareness of how our bodies and minds work. Much more on this later.

From the awareness of self, we begin to work on making sense of the world. How do things work? How do I fit into the world?

What Is Truth?

Initially, our world is mostly made up of home and family. As we grow, our world expands. There is not only more in which to become aware, but the questions about how things work and how do I fit become larger.

We can now circle back to our first construct. How does **truth** and **not-truth** link up with this construct? I would think that it would be obvious that if we reach conclusions about who we are and how the world works based upon **truth**, we are in a far better place than if our conclusions are based on **not-truth**.

Now let's make this concept of how the world works a little more complex but hopefully clearer. When we introduce the truth as revealed in the Bible, we discover that there is a system called the world and a system called the Kingdom of God. Here is the distinction between the two: Those who are born again, children of God, and who have received Jesus are in the Kingdom of God, and those who are not believers are not in the Kingdom of God. Since both the world and Kingdom of God are in existence at the same time, the believer has the advantage of making sense of the world about them that the unbeliever does not because the believer is coming from a position of **truth**.

Although believers are in the world, they are not of the world. When the believer seeks to answer the self-awareness questions, they have answers based upon biblical **truth**. Believers understand that they were created by God; as children of God, they are family members with many benefits. When believers look at things and people around them, they know that these were created by God.

They can use the Bible as the reliable source of **truth** to learn about who God is and what He has done and is doing. They discover Jesus and the multiple benefits that are provided through His redemptive work. Believers also learn that God has placed the Holy Spirit within them to guide them into all truth. Dallas Willard identifies these basic questions: "What kind of world do we live in? and How does God relate to us, confined as we are within it?"

The believer is in a much better position to make sense of who they are and how the world works than the unbeliever. Let's remember this awareness is something that is developmental and progressive. Awareness and commitment to the **truth** is the essential path to making accurate sense of who we are and how the world works.

Before we move on to the next construct, let's pause and reflect on the Lord Jesus and His self-system. Jesus knew exactly who He was and what His mission was. My favorite example of this is the washing of the disciples' feet (John 13). The scriptures say—and this is my paraphrase—Jesus being fully cognizant of who He was and where He came from, arose from the table and took a towel and a bowl and began to wash the disciples' feet. Jesus also declared his mission; to heal the broken hearted and set the captives free. (Luke 4:18)

So much to figure out: **truth** and **not-truth**, "who am I?", "how does the world work?", "where does God fit into all of this?", "what am I supposed to do?" There is a need for more clues!

Chapter 5

Our Brain

The whole self-awareness and making sense of the world takes place in our brains—one of those self-evident truths that we may not think about very often.

Now, on to the next construct! Remember I mentioned at this time in our existence we have a body. I am sure that you are aware that we are fearfully and wonderfully made. Scripture makes it clear that these bodies are temporary and a new body awaits us. What will the new bodies be like? More mystery!

Looking more closely at our brain, we recognize that it is the control center. So many of our systems, many which are involuntary, are linked to the brain; think of it, the nervous system, the circulatory system, the digestive system, the respiratory system, sight, smell, taste, and hearing—all wonderful, but we are going to focus on the mind.

The mind is private and personal. Only we truly know our thoughts. A friend and mentor of mine, Jim Wright, would say that we can observe and make some judgments on peoples' behaviors, but only God knows their hearts. I have no idea what you are thinking as you read this, and you have no idea what I am thinking as I write it. You may assume that I am thinking about what I am writing—but what else?

Let's look a little closer at how our God-given brain works. An aside—how many can remember a parent's strong exhortation, "Why don't you use the brain God gave you?" Our brains operate on a continuum from survival to prosperity. Fundamentally, our brain is critical to survival.

Although we do some thinking in pictures primarily we think in words. That is why we teach children to speak. It is understood that the greater the vocabulary, the greater the potential for deeper thinking and understanding. Linking back to the self-system we understand that the development of the self-system is connected to learning and we use our brain to learn.

Let's pause to listen to Oswald Chambers from *My Utmost for His Highest*:

> Jesus said: "The words that I speak unto you," not the words I have spoken, "they are spirit, and they are life." The Bible has been so many words to us—clouds and darkness—then all of a sudden the words become spirit and life because Jesus re-speaks them to us in a particular condition. That is the way God speaks to us, not by visions and dreams, but by words. When a man gets to God it is by the most simple way of words.

More and more scientists, physicians, and educators are learning further truths about the structure of the brain and how it works. Here I want to present a disclaimer. These sources may or may not be the truth—not that there is necessarily an intention to mislead or deceive—but the knowledge about how the brain works is a work in progress, and some earlier conclusions are being revised and disputed.

For example, the strong positions on right and left hemisphere functions that were all the rage at one time are now being revised.

Our Brain

My main point is the information about brain function as currently held is not as soundly in the truth column as the Word of God is.

We know the brain processes information that our body receives through our senses. The experts believe that our brains have the capacity to receive and process vast amounts of information very quickly. As these inputs flood into our brain, our sensory register sorts the inputs and moves some of the inputs into our short-term memory. Mostly we are not aware of this process because most of the inputs are not particularly relevant. Remember the first sort of the inputs will be linked to survival.

Let me pause and illustrate: Back in the early 60s, my brother and I were spraying wild iris in a meadow. The wild iris plants were invasive and a problem for the rancher. Our spray rig was an open jeep that pulled a trailer with a tank containing the herbicide. One guy drove the jeep while the other guy walked around dragging a hose with a spray nozzle. As a normal part of the process, the guy driving the jeep would move up and stop as needed to keep the spraying guy with the necessary hose to reach the plants.

Of course, as the driver moved the jeep, the hose would move and flop. Normally this is no big deal, but the ranch hand who had given us directions on where to spray happened to mention that recently they had killed several rattlesnakes near where we would be going. This new information registered in our brains and connected to the survival mode so as the guy operating the spray gun moved from plant to plant where his focus was, out of the corner of his eye he would catch the movement of the hose as it was dragged and flopped when the jeep moved.

Now the routine movement of the hose suddenly could be perceived to possibly be a snake moving. I remember being startled and it seemed that my heart jumped into my throat. The sorting done by the sensory register was looking out for us.

How the Brain Works

The experts believe that the information moved to the short-term memory is only there for a little while and some of it is moved through working memory to the long-term memory where it is stored. The goal of learning is to get the important stuff to the long-term memory. Another model used to describe brain function is sensory memory—working memory and permanent memory. Either model works. It is important to point out that everything ending up in the long term or permanent memory is not necessarily the truth, however ideally we want it to be!

Let's look more closely at how this processing works. The initial inputs that come into our sensory register come in as details—lots of details. The details are sorted and organized into categories in our working memory. In our working memory, the categories are elaborated upon and connected with prior knowledge that is located in our permanent memory.

Essentially, the working memory goes into permanent memory to gather this prior knowledge for elaboration of the information, and finally, the working memory explores the permanent memory to discover stored information that will establish evidence that the information is accurate.

Wow! That can give a person a headache, and I didn't even use the many fifty-dollar words that the experts do to label parts of the brain. Let's use a real-life experience to see if we can understand this process a little better.

During lambing season, I observed one ewe who was not acting right. I mentioned it to my wife, Karen, and she had observed the same thing. Our observation consisted of seeing that the ewe was not eating normally and seemed kind of dull. She was not rejecting her lamb but was not being attentive. This is not normal behavior.

Here is what was happening in our brains. First, through sight we saw the details of the ewe's behavior and sorted those details into categories in our working memory. Then our working memory went into our permanent memory to elaborate the information in the category and to search for evidence in the permanent memory from prior experiences to support our conclusion that something was wrong.

Our collaboration about our observations used our shared permanent memory to verify our conclusions. However, we were not through using our brains because now we had a problem to solve—what to do about this ewe who was not acting normally.

Once again, our working memory took a trip into our permanent memory and found that in the past, we had contacted our veterinarian. Since Karen had the vet's phone number in her phone, she called and made arrangements for Dr. Tyler Ratzlaff to come and look at the ewe. When Tyler arrived, he observed the ewe, taking in the details of her behavior and moving them into his working memory where they could be put in categories. Then his working memory could elaborate on the information and go into his permanent memory to compare with information stored there.

Tyler proceeded to use his stethoscope to listen to her heart and breathing and also took her temperature. Tyler used his working memory to go into his permanent memory to access what he had learned about processes for diagnosing and what normal breathing should sound like and what would be normal body temperatures.

Again, using this information his working memory again accessed his permanent memory to come up with the diagnosis of pneumonia. Once again, he went into his permanent memory to gather information about what medication to use. He also was able to call upon permanent memory to know how to administer the medication.

This illustration is almost finished, but as we talked about the situation, Karen and I, as well as Tyler recalled how a few years before we had a pneumonia outbreak and lost several lambs. Tyler had helped us with that problem. We accessed that memory, using our working memory to go into our permanent memory. We also remembered that probably this ewe had been held as a replacement ewe from that group of lambs.

Tyler's permanent memory revealed that even though this ewe had not died from the pneumonia, she likely had had a touch of it and the tendency is for there to be a weakness toward future troubles with pneumonia. Now this elaboration on the processing was not conscious on any of our parts, but it does illustrate how our brains process.

You may be wondering, why all this brain processing stuff? How does it relate? Please be patient because I want you to remember that these constructs are scaffolded to build an important construct. These explanations of brain processing have been very mechanical, but please remember this is happening at a very rapid pace.

We never even examined the role of emotions in the whole process. Examining emotions is not critical to the part of processing we explored, but you can be sure that all three of us, Karen, Tyler, and I, had emotions related to the ewe and each other.

Let's go back to the construct of **truth** and **not-truth**. Truth is made of principles, formulas, axioms, and propositions. The truths are universal and are always true. For many years I have indulged myself with the practice of analyzing content I am learning in courses, in reading, in trainings, in the news, or peoples' comments to see if they match up with biblical principles as I understand them. My conclusion is the content that lines up with biblical principles work, and I think that is why this construct works. This is an example of a biblical world view.

We keep seeing that our analysis of the mystery of godliness and our search for clues reveals that becoming godly and Christ-like is a process. The process has a beginning at personal salvation but advances through the development of relationship with the Lord Jesus. We have just explored how our brain functions in the *"renewing of our minds"*—a part of the process.

Chapter 6

Belief Drives Practice

> "Hence, if we would train people to do "all things," we must change their beliefs. Only so we can change their loves. You cannot change character or behavior and leave beliefs intact."
> Dallas Willard from *Divine Conspiracy,* page 331.

Keeping in mind our exploration of how the brain God gave us works, let's look at another construct. This construct is a formula. Simply stated it is: "Belief Drives Practice." Looking closer, we see belief takes place in our minds (brains). Belief is linked to faith. The believer chorus says, "Faith is just believing what God says is true." Perhaps faith and belief are interchangeable, but I want to use the word belief.

Although both words, faith and belief, appear many times in scripture, I am concerned that in our culture the word faith sometimes becomes spiritualized and ritualized. For example, I think for many the Lord's Prayer has become so ritualized that many if not most people don't grasp the significance and power of it.

I have read accounts where commentators have unpacked the Lord's Prayer to reveal the power and wonder of it. Even though faith and belief are synonyms, that is why I want to use the word belief.

Belief Drives Practice

My tendency is to think that either you have a belief, or you don't have a belief. When I reflect upon my own issues about belief, I test myself with the question: Do you believe or not? However, scripture indicates there is a quantifying factor for faith and belief. It is not quite as black and white as I sometimes want to make it. There is strong and weak belief.

There appears to be a continuum for belief or faith and strong belief or faith is a good and desirable thing. That being the case, we can conclude that strong belief will generate a stronger drive that will result in a stronger practice. Here are some verses that support the continuum of intensity idea because we see great faith, strong faith, increasing faith, and growth in faith.

When Jesus heard it, he marvelled, and said to them that followed, Verily I say unto you, I have not found so great faith, no, not in Israel (Matthew 8:10).

Then Jesus answered and said unto her, O woman, great is thy faith: be it unto thee even as thou wilt. And her daughter was made whole from that very hour (Matthew 15:28).

Ever since I first heard of your strong faith in the Lord Jesus and your love for God's people everywhere (Ephesians 1:15 NLT).

And the apostles said unto the Lord, Increase our faith (Luke 17:5).

We are bound to thank God always for you, brethren, as it is meet, because that your faith groweth exceedingly, and the charity of every one of you all toward each other aboundeth (II Thessalonians 1:3).

We are not bragging beyond measure about other people's

labors. But we have the hope that as your faith increases, our area of ministry will be greatly enlarged (II Corinthians 10: 15).

Believe What?

Another consideration as we look closer at belief and faith is that belief and faith have an object. When we believe, we are believing something or in something. When we say we believe, the obvious question is: What do you believe or in what or whom do you believe? This may seem very obvious, but it is important and helpful to be able to clearly state what you believe.

That is why we call ourselves believers. Believers believe in the Lord Jesus Christ, His saving work, His promise, His Word, and the truths that are being discussed here. A fair question for us to repeatedly ask ourselves is: What do I believe?

Let's pause and look at comments on faith by Dallas Willard:

> Faith is not opposed to knowledge; faith is opposed to sight. And grace is not opposed to effort; it is opposed to earning. Commitment is not sustained by confusion but by insight. The person who is uninformed and confused will inevitably be unstable and vulnerable in action, thought and feeling. (*Hearing God*, p. 254).

For we walk by faith, not by sight (II Corinthians 5:7).

Recall that our thoughts and memories are private and personal. We also may not be really aware of what we believe, but we do believe something. This believing has to do with each situation and event in our lives.

The construct of belief drives practice sounds like a formula and in many ways, it is. However, to better understand it, I think we should explore some of the nuances related to it. Formulas are rather mechanical. Input data out comes results. For example: A=LxW. You probably recognize that as the formula for the area of a rectangle. Insert a value for (L) length and a value for (W) width, do the math, and you find (A) area in square units. This can easily be demonstrated by drawing a model on graph paper and counting the squares. It always works and it is reliable.

A recipe is another kind of formula. All you have to do to reach your desired results is to, as we say, follow the recipe. Be sure to put in the correct ingredients in the proper amounts and follow the directions and the end result is a delicious pie or cake, for example. This is all very straightforward and mechanical. When the dish does not turn out as expected, there is an immediate question: Did you follow the recipe?

One of the nuances on our "belief drives practice" construct is often we do not think very much about what we believe when we make decisions that will activate the drive part of the formula. Let me use a very simple illustration. As I am typing, I am also drinking my morning cup of coffee. From time to time I pause, pick up my cup, and take a sip. Taking a sip is the practice part of the formula. I know this is very simple and mundane, but it illustrates an activity in which I really don't think much about my beliefs that drive the practice of sipping coffee. I think if I did, it would be kind of weird.

However, for this illustration I am going to reflect on some beliefs around my cup of coffee. I believe that my coffee tastes good, and it gives me pleasure. I believe that it is great way to start my day. I know people who do not drink coffee, and as strange as it sounds to me, they say they don't like the taste. Consciously thinking

The Mystery of Godliness

about what we believe is probably rather rare, but it does not mean that the belief does not exist. It exists!

Before we explore more on this nuance about believing, let's look at another more complex example. Here is the story: My brother-in-law is a radio engineer who works on the technical equipment in many radio stations. Because he has done so for many years, he fits my definition of an expert. From time to time he does work for some local radio stations near where we live. He and my sister come to our house often and stay overnight while he is working here.

I frequently go with him to work on the station. I have titled myself as his Incompetent Assistant, which is an accurate definition. He has shortened my title to an acronym: I.A. My assisting usually only amounts to a little fetching of tools and occasionally taking something apart. I have no desire to ever do what he does, but I am curious and like to see what he is doing and learn what I can. I have come away very impressed with all the complicated workings behind the scenes in radio broadcasting, but let's get to the point.

Often the project for the day is to troubleshoot a problem of something not working correctly. Believe me, there are a lot of things that could be wrong because there are so many pieces. There are issues about power levels and frequencies that need to be within certain tolerances. My brother-in-law has a number of expensive tools that can be plugged into the equipment to get readings. Then there are dials and meters that need to be adjusted. It is really complicated, but my brother-in-law systematically goes about a diagnostic process to find the adjustment that needs to be made or discover a part that is not functioning properly.

He is very good about telling me what he is doing and why, and if he doesn't tell, I ask. Mostly I don't really understand very well what he is telling me, but it is interesting.

Finally, I am going to get to the point! As my brother-in-law goes through the step by step process of taking readings with his nifty expensive machines, he is following his belief about what might be wrong. Sometimes he even says, I believe such and such may not be set right or such and such may not be working (those terms such and such are as close as I can get to the technical language).

His belief is based upon his knowledge of what proper settings should be or how certain components should be working. Proper settings and proper functioning of components represent the truth. My brother-in-law is using his belief in these truths to drive his practice of doing diagnostic practices. Upon discovering the trouble and moving to correcting the problem, once again he will use his belief in the truth of correct setting and proper functioning to drive the practice of adjustments or replacement.

Now I really am going to get to the point. In this very complex illustration, there is very little awareness of the belief that is actually driving the practice. The nuance simply stated is: there does not need to be an awareness of the truth for the construct to work. When we apply this understanding to our journey to godliness, we can understand that as the truth becomes part of our belief system, we will move to godly practice.

Collision

Let's look at what happens when **truth** and **not-truth** collide. When **truth** and **not-truth** collide, a decision is initiated. The decision is whether to submit to the truth or rebel against the truth. This sounds kind of harsh and severe. We can say it another way. The decision is whether to accept the truth or reject it. This sounds a little less harsh, but it doesn't really matter how we state it. What are our options?

Stick with me now because the next few sentences are challenging. If we choose to submit to the truth or accept the truth, it becomes part of our belief system. This belief in the truth will drive our practice. If we choose to rebel against the truth or reject the truth, it becomes part of our belief system. This belief in the truth will drive our practice.

If we choose to submit to the **not-truth** or accept the **not-truth**, it becomes part of our belief system. This belief in the **not-truth** will drive our practice. If we choose to rebel against the **not-truth** or reject the **not-truth,** it becomes part of our belief system. This belief in the **not-truth** will drive our practice. We have explored all decision options for when **truth** and **not-truth** collide.

The bottom line is that we choose what we are going to believe and what we are not going to believe. This fits in nicely with what we all experience—life is a series of choices and decisions.

This also fits nicely with understanding the scriptures because the scripture offers choices, warns of bad choices, and gives many examples of people who have made good and bad choices. Clearly, we want to make wise choices, and wise choices are based on believing the truth. Can you see that our will is involved? Because we have choices, accountability is appropriate. Consequences—good or bad—also are appropriate. This is how the world works both in and out of the Kingdom of God. This also impacts our determination of who we are. Doesn't it all really make sense?

Another nuance to consider is that our focus needs to be on believing the truth. If our focus is on belief, the practice will follow.

There is no need to try to force the practice because the energy for the practice comes from the belief. The belief will determine the decisions that will drive the practice. Simply put, if you believe it you will figure it out.

If you believe the truth about who you are and how you work, you will figure out the practice. Now for an example: If you believe that the Lord wants you to be kind, and you want to please Him by being kind, you will figure out how to practice kindness. Opportunities will come along in which you will be able to act in a kind matter and show kindness. In some ways this takes the work out of being kind. It will just happen.

Hence, the commandments of the Lord are not grievous. I John 5:3 says, *"For this is the love of God, that we keep his commandments: and his commandments are not grievous."* You find that being kind is not hard. As a matter of fact, it is easy and natural. It becomes so easy and natural that you are hardly aware of being kind. In fact, you would not even consider being unkind. This is godly behavior and evidence of a transformed life and renewed mind.

Oops—a Miss

One more nuance to explore. Sometimes two people or two groups of people can be holding a truth as a belief, and yet in their communication they do not agree. The two opposing views are usually talking about different beliefs, and the two parties are not really hearing the context of the other's beliefs. These differences can cause disruption and in some cases strife. The strife can even get out of hand and turn to violence. Certainly, if left unresolved, alienation can occur. Here is a story that is a good illustration of such an occurrence.

Many years ago, when I was in high school, I was in an agriculture class. The way the program was designed was that freshmen had a one-hour class, and sophomores through seniors had a two-hour class. Students would spend two days each week working in the shop and three days each week in the classroom. Our instructor was Mr. Kelly. I really liked him, and it is my impression that my classmates also liked him.

Mr. Kelly's students were all farm boys, and at the time part of the course requirement was that every student had to have an agricultural related project, either livestock or crops. Part of the curriculum was record keeping on the students' projects. From a teacher's perspective, there were some positives related to the nature of the students.

Since all the students were living on a farm and most had grown up on a farm, the students had considerable background knowledge. For the same reasons, the content of the course was relevant to the students. From an instructional standpoint this is good because the students have both background knowledge and the content is relevant. In other instructional settings, the effective teacher must build the background knowledge and somehow find a way to make the content relevant to the student. All of this story background is for the purpose of setting the stage for the conflict.

One of the standards in Mr. Kelly's instruction was the concept of "approved practice." It seemed that whatever the topic of study the class was pursuing, there was the conclusion of what constituted approved practice. Most of the approved practice was readily accepted by the class, but every once in a while, an approved practice did not match what was actually happening on some students' farms.

This could set the stage for a conflict between Mr. Kelly's ap-

Belief Drives Practice

proved practice and someone's father's actual practice. I don't remember that this happened very often, and when it did, it usually led to some kind of constructive discussion.

Now the stage is set, so let's finally look at the incident that is the point of the story. I have to confess that I probably was the instigator of the conflict that developed and also that my memory from an event that happened so long ago may not be completely accurate. But here is the issue: I observed and was supported by most of my classmates that when pasture/hay meadows had been burned off, the grass greened up earliest in the spring. Where the fire had burned, the grass was greener and growing earlier than in the surrounding area that was not burned and blackened.

However, burning off grass is not an approved practice. There is sound reasoning behind not burning off the grass. Burning destroys organic matter in the thatch and stubble that eventually decomposes and provides nourishment to the grass. The conflict arose as I remember it over the fact that Mr. Kelly was very protective of his approved practices. So, a clash occurred between the observed response of the grass to burning as opposed to the approved practice of not burning.

As I recall the contention, although not really hostile but fervent, lasted for several days. It seemed clear to me that the precepts, "to burn" or "not to burn," were not really in conflict because the "to burn" was just an observation, not something that was to be advocated while the "not to burn" was clearly an approved practice to be advocated. We had two truths being proclaimed.

There was not a need for them to be contested, and yet they were contested. I can remember asserting that my position was not opposed to Mr. Kelly's position, but it seemed to him to an affront to his position of approved practice. In reflection I believe I could have been more respectful and dropped the whole issue.

The point is sixty years later I still clearly remember the encounter. The long-term implication and lesson is that division and strife can occur when two different truths are held by two different individuals or groups and can be assumed to be in opposition when they really are not. The challenge is for each person, in their search for a commitment, to identify the truth and then commit to believing that truth and to be sure when an opposing view appears that it really is not just another truth.

Drives—Practices

Now let's explore the term, "drives." In this part of the formula, our will comes in play because we make choices and decisions and these are based on our beliefs. Another way to think of it is that drives put the beliefs into actions. Several times in Romans, Paul uses the word "reckoning" which I think works for drives. Dallas Willard describes this reckoning as "to think in a certain way and to count upon things being as we then think of them."

What do we mean by "practice"? The practice is the actions demonstrated by behaviors. These practices can be in thought, word, or deed.

Let's go back and explore belief a little deeper. We can believe wrong things or not believe the right thing. Simple example: Eve believed Satan's lie, which drove her to the practice of eating the forbidden fruit. She acted on her belief.

Reviewing the sick ewe event and thinking about the participants, Karen, Tyler and I all worked out of our belief system. Karen and I had beliefs about what a healthy ewe should look like. We had be-

Belief Drives Practice

liefs about Tyler's capacity to help. These beliefs drove us to the action (practice) of contacting Tyler and asking for help. Tyler had a belief that he could help, which drove him to come to the farm. Tyler also had a belief about the effectiveness of the medication, which drove him to use it. We could go back through the whole brain processing explanation about this event and find further examples of beliefs driving practices, but this should be enough.

Belief does not require understanding. There just needs to be confidence that the belief is true. Karen and I did not need to understand all that Tyler knew or how the medication worked. All we had to do was believe in Tyler, and that belief is what drove us to contact him (practice). However, understanding can enrich and strengthen belief. Many times we have probably said, "Now I understand it, so now I can believe it."

I am guessing that by now you have gathered that the formula "belief drives practice" not only is a primary clue to solving our mystery, but that it is lurking in the background of all the other clues we have explored and will be exploring. If we can grasp its importance, we will see this formula applies again and again in what we are seeing and doing. Keep watching for it!

Chapter 7

Believers Applying Belief Drives Practice

"We really come to think and believe differently, and that changes everything" (Dallas Willard from *Divine Conspiracy* p. 362).

Now let's apply the construct of "Belief Drives Practice" to the life of faith for the believer. This application is the real point to everything that has been said up to now. The information generally is helpful in guiding a person to understand themselves and how the world works, but its real value is assisting us to understand how this all works in the process of the believer being conformed to the image of Christ.

It is helpful for believers, as we become more and more Christ-like, that we understand the "Belief Drives Practice" formula is working. What is critical is what we believe. If we believe the truth that God proclaimed, the formula begins to work because the truth-based belief will drive our practice, and our practice will be Christ-like. If our belief is based on God's proclaimed truth, we do not need further evidence. This is in contrast to the court cases where the sworn witnesses are part of a search for the truth.

God's truth may not always be visible or understandable. It is not

Believers Applying Belief Drives Practice

vital that believers understand something that God has said before they believe it. It is enough that God has said it because the basis for the belief is confidence in God. So, we can stand firmly on the proposition that we not only believe in God, but also we believe what He says.

When we believe God, the drive part of the formula becomes "obey." We can rephrase the formula as: "Belief in God's Word drives obedience, resulting in a righteous practice" The believer walks by faith not by sight. The believer is not requiring evidence. God's proclamation is all that is needed for evidence. If the miraculous could be explained, it would not be miraculous. *"...without controversy great is the mystery of godliness"* (I Timothy 3:16).

Jerry Bridges says in his book *The Practice of Godliness*:

> In Titus 1:1 Paul refers to "the knowledge of the truth that leads to godliness." We cannot grow in godliness without the knowledge of the truth. This truth is to be found only in the Bible, but it is not just academic knowledge of Bible facts. It is spiritual knowledge taught by the Holy Spirit as he applies the truth of God to our hearts. (p. 45)

Earlier I referred to the many benefits for believers. The believer is not left on his own to discern the truth to believe. God's plan for His children included sending a guide for discerning the truth. He sent the Comforter, the Holy Spirit, to dwell in us and to lead us into all truth.

God in us is an amazing part of the mystery of godliness. As we develop our own self-awareness, a critical part of that awareness is that God, the Holy Spirit, is dwelling in us. We are sealed by the Holy Spirit.

> *In whom ye also trusted, after that ye heard the word of truth, the gospel of your salvation: in whom also after that ye believed, ye were sealed with that Holy Spirit of promise* (Ephesians 1:13).

By the Holy Spirit, God is able to speak directly to us. This benefit assists us in understanding how the world works. We know that we are in a world at war. There is a battle with the devil, the flesh, and the world system (more on this later). We have a righteous role in that battle. God has a purpose for each of us.

Wow! How richly blessed the believer is! We know and believe that God is love and His actions are driven to demonstrate that love. In His love we have great safety because His perfect love casts out fear. *"There is no fear in love; but perfect love casteth out fear"* (I John 4:18). *"For God hath not given us the spirit of fear; but of power, and of love, and of a sound mind"* (II Timothy 1:7). God's truth provides the answers we are seeking in order to understand how the world works and how the Kingdom of God fits into that explanation.

Proof

Let's pause and look further at how the "Belief Drives Practice" works. Let's see what it looks like. Do you believe that God loves you? Do you believe that you love God? The Lord Jesus boiled down the commandments from God into these two: Love God and love your neighbor. The Good Samaritan story made it clear that our neighbor is other people. Jesus also said if you love Me, you will obey Me. Think about it; if you love God and obey Him, your practice will be affected. If you love your neighbor, your practice will be affected.

Here are a couple of story illustrations. The husband and father in the family of our Amish neighbors had a sudden situation in which

Believers Applying Belief Drives Practice

his mother was dying back in Michigan, and they were called to go there. It just happened to be right at the time of the second hay cutting, not a good time for him to be gone.

Karen and I were walking out to bring our horses in from grazing south of our house. It was around nine o'clock in the morning. All of a sudden, we saw a string of Amish neighbors coming with their teams and swathers. (A swather is a machine used to cut hay, and the Amish use teams of horses rather than tractors.) There were five or six of them. Capture the scene as it unfolds: First, we see one team and swather, then here comes another one, and as we look down the road here come another and another. They swooped in on the alfalfa field, and by four o'clock in the afternoon the field was cut; one by one they returned to their homes. I confess I had tears and every time I tell the story I get tears.

What a great demonstration of loving your neighbor! Shortly after this I was talking with one of those who had been part of the group and telling him how much I was touched by the demonstration of loving your neighbor. His simple response was, "That is what we do." The belief to love your neighbor drove these people to the practice of mowing their neighbor's alfalfa.

A caution here: remember when I said we can judge behaviors and only God can judge hearts. It is possible that not all of those who participated were motivated by a belief in loving their neighbor, but I am comfortable assuming that they did love their neighbor.

Here's another story with the same Amish neighbor, but it has to do with haying. An aside, this neighbor showed neighborly love to us by bring us a load of firewood when I was laid up after having a knee replaced.

The Mystery of Godliness

Now, back to the story. This man was working on getting his hay put up and had been interrupted several times by rain. He had everything baled except for about 10-15% of the field. Finally, it was dry enough to finish baling, but the storm clouds were building and it was threatening to rain. He was out with his team working on finishing baling. I noticed that he suddenly quit, and I was wondering what was happening and thought maybe something broke on the baler.

Then I received a phone call from these neighbors. Their teenage son was not feeling well, and they were concerned about a possible blood clot. They called and asked I if could take them to the emergency room to have him checked out, and could I pick them up in about half an hour? I said that I could, and I had a chance to love my neighbor, but that is not the story here.

As I was getting ready to go pick them up to go to the emergency room, I saw two tractors with balers descend on the alfalfa field and begin baling up the remaining windrows. Think about the contrast of speed with which the hay gets baled when the bailer is pulled by a team of horses or when it is pulled by a large tractor. By the time I arrived to pick them up to go to the emergency room, the tractors had finished up the field just before it began to rain.

Here is what happened: a neighbor who farms next door happened to stop by their house and learned about the emergency situation. He called his brother and the two of them proceeded to bale up the field. These neighbors demonstrated love for their neighbors. It was a beautiful sight to see. (Also, the son did not have a clot.)

These are just two examples of observing practices that indicated a person had the belief of loving their neighbors. As I thought of these two stories, my mind was flooded with other examples. Since

Believers Applying Belief Drives Practice

we cannot see into the hearts of others we can't be sure of their beliefs, but we can see their practices.

Here is one more short story that demonstrated to me the practice of those who love God. Many years ago, I had the opportunity and privilege to attend a Promise Keepers event at the old Mile High Stadium in Denver. The stadium was packed with men who were demonstrating a love for God.

There is no way for me to know what was in anyone's heart but when thousands of men sang "Amazing Grace," I think I could smell heaven. I sang through tears and have tears as I tell this story. The practice of this large audience of men reflected their belief in a love for God.

James 1:22 says, *"Be ye doers of the word and not hearers only."* Between hearing and doing is believing and obeying. The doing is the practice. Here is some good news: the starting point is believing and the end point is practice. We can easily get things turned around. Since the practice is visible and probably desirable, we can be tempted through some self-effort to just do it by our own will power. We may not even consider what we actually believe.

The key is that the formula is automatic. If we believe right, we will act right. Our emphasis needs to be on what we believe. What if we realize that our practice is not what we want? In other words, we do not like what we are doing or how we are acting. This happens and happens a lot.

Obviously, when this happens it may be appropriate to repent and apologize for what we have been doing and it may be appropriate to ask forgiveness from someone, but this awareness is an opportunity to explore our thinking and believing. This is part of figuring out how things work, particularly as a member of the kingdom of God. Once again, it is a process!

Chapter 8

When People Believe Not-Truth

In the beginning God created the heaven and the earth. And the earth was without form, and void; and darkness was upon the face of the deep. And the Spirit of God moved upon the face of the waters (Genesis 1:1-2).

Now I want to explore an example from the Bible of how a wrong belief drives practice. This is a not a clue for understanding the mystery of godliness, but sometimes looking at a negative example can be helpful to increase understanding. This example I think is particularly helpful in understanding the world we are living in today. The passage I want to consider comes from Romans1:18-20.

For the wrath of God is revealed from heaven against all ungodliness and unrighteousness of men, who hold the truth in unrighteousness; Because that which may be known of God hath shewed it unto them. For the invisible things of Him from the creation of the world are clearly seen, being understood by the things that are made, even his eternal power and Godhead; so that they are without excuse.

Why is it so important to acknowledge the creation? Tozer says:

The teaching of the New Testament is that God created the world by the Logos, the Word, and the Word is identified with the second Person of the Godhead who was present in the world! even before He became incarnate in human nature. The Word made all things and remained in His creation to uphold and sustain it and be at the same time a moral light enabling every man to distinguish good from evil. The universe operates as an orderly system, not by impersonal laws but by the creative voice of the immanent and universal Presence, the Logos (*Knowledge of the Holy*, p. 81)

In another place Tozer says:

> Without the creation, the wisdom of God would have remained forever locked in the boundless abyss of the divine nature. God brought His creatures into being that He might enjoy them and they rejoice in Him. "And God saw everything that he had made, and, behold, it was very good" (p. 67).

> *Who is the image of the invisible God, the firstborn of every creature: For by him were all things created, that are in heaven, and that are in earth, visible and invisible, whether they be thrones, or dominions, or principalities, or powers: all things were created by him, and for him. And he is before all things, and by him, all things consist* (Colossians 1:15-17).

Before we proceed, notice Tozer mentioned the wisdom of God. Let's review one of our mysteries from early in Chapter 1.

> *But we speak the wisdom of God in a **mystery**, even the hidden wisdom, which God ordained before the world unto glory: Which none of the princes of this world knew: for had they known it, they would not have crucified the Lord of glory* (I Corinthians 2:7-8 author emphasis).

Seeing the Invisible

Think about this. God's creation is visible. It is all around us. We see it. We touch it. We are part of it. Acknowledging God as the Creator and the creation as a work of God provides a transition from sight to faith. Ponder this verse:

> *For we walk by faith, not by sight* (II Corinthians 5:7).

When People Believe Not-Truth

Follow me! Since faith is based on believing what God says, there is no need to rely on sight. But God in His gentle mercy has provided creation as a visible evidence of the invisible divine nature to provide that transition to faith. When we see the beauty and utility of creation, we begin to grasp the divine nature of God and the natural response will be thankfulness.

Everyone is without excuse for not knowing God's eternal power and divine nature by observing creation. But how can we see the invisible? In this case, seeing the invisible character of God. Actually, we do this all the time. Follow me with this series of illustrations. At our house my wife, Karen, does almost all the meal preparation, which is a good thing for me. Most of the time, I am not very aware of what she is doing. She has shopped for the food, she has planned the meal, she has done all the work of preparing it, and then she often serves it. I get to enjoy it.

The invisible that I do see is how she has in a very caring manner gone through all the necessary steps to provide me with a very tasty meal using invisible knowledge and skill and demonstrating her love for me. She also always prepares food that I like. One of the ways I know that these extra measures are for my benefit is she has told me about how she eats when she is alone. It is much simpler. I see these invisible qualities in the practice and product.

From time to time we go out to an upscale restaurant to eat, usually for a special occasion. You can tell the restaurant is upscale by the tablecloths on the tables and the attractive centerpiece. The menu provides another clue because the items are printed in a fancy font, there are no pictures, and the prices are rounded off, $19-$23. When the food is served, it will be on large heavy plates, and there are sprigs of green herbs or slivers of carrot decorating the dish. The ambiance is very impressive. The invisible things about the chef are clearly seen, although the chef is rarely seen. The chef cares about presentation of the food. Care is taken to make sure everything is prepared carefully and the food is placed just right on the plate. Also, the chef knows what he is doing.

Usually we catch a quick bite at Wendy's. This is very different. We order off the menu that is posted on the wall. There is often pictures of the food and the prices include the cents—$3.79-$4.99. We give them our name, and our name is called when the order is ready, which is usually not very long. When the number is called, you pick up your tray, self-serve for condiments and napkins and straws, find an available table, seat yourself, and unwrap your food order. Upon completing the meal, you bus your own table and leave.

What about the person who prepared the meal? They are not really visible, but sometimes you can kind of see them working in the back of the restaurant. They are quickly and sometime frantically cooking and wrapping the food. My conclusion about their invisible qualities is that they are pushing to be fast, uniform, and not particularly concerned about me, the customer. This is okay because the mission of Wendy's is to be fast, efficient, and consistent.

My last example of seeing the invisible has to do with my preparing a meal for Karen and me. This does not happen often, but it has become a tradition. My specialty and pretty much only meal has been previously prepared by Marie Calendar. Marie has prepared these tasty meals in nice packages and frozen them.

Marie has also conveniently provided microwave directions on the back of the packages. I simply read them and follow them and shortly there is a hot meal in its own plastic container. The containers are black, and I suspect that the black color microwaves better. I serve the meal with gentle politeness and provide a fork, a knife if necessary, a napkin, and a salt shaker. I seek to present it in a classy way. After the meal is over I clear the plastic container, utensils, and used napkins. I throw the plastic container in the trash and put the fork in the dishwasher.

There you see I have prepared the meal and done the dishes. What does this say about my invisible character? I let you draw your own conclusions. The point is we all see invisible things all the time.

Consequences

Now back to our verse and the point of people being without excuse. Romans 1:21-22 go on to say:

> *Because that, when they knew God, they glorified him not as God, neither were thankful, but became vain in their imaginations, and their foolish hearts were darkened. Professing themselves to be wise, they became fools.*

The rest of the chapter goes on to elaborate on the impact of their darkened foolish hearts, resulting in many unseemly and wicked practices. The last verse of the chapter says they also have pleasure in others who are doing these wicked practices.

This is a long chapter and we are going to get into some pretty heavy stuff. I want to pause to explain why I have chosen these passages to serve as negative examples of belief drives practice because of believing a **not-truth** and simultaneously denying a **truth.** The belief in evolution as an explanation of origins is pervasive in our culture. What began as a theory is not clearly assumed to be a fact. I have found Dallas Willard's explanation of culture and how it relates to our belief systems helpful, and I think you will too.

The Mystery of Godliness

Culture is seen in what people do unthinkingly, what is "natural" to them and therefore requires no explanation or justification. Everyone has a culture—or, really, multidimensional cultures of various levels. These cultures structure their lives. And of course by far the most of everyone's culture is right and good and essential. But not all. For culture is the place where wickedness takes on group form, just as the flesh, good and right in itself, is the place where individual wickedness dwells (*Divine Conspiracy*, page 260).

The desirable culture for the person seeking to be godly is a culture that is set around a biblical world view. I find it important to remind us of this truth once again before we proceed into the darkness of this example of believing **not-truth.**

I want to focus on vain imaginations and professing themselves to be wise. People are fascinated about origins. Just look at all the interests in ancestry as evidenced by the ads on television for ancestry.com. Some people work very hard to construct a family tree.

The fascination with origins is common to all of us. In the early stages of conversation with a new acquaintance, it often includes questions about where the other person came from. The answer could include recent places that the person has lived or even where they were born. Sometimes the answer could include the country of origin of the person's ancestors. Often people who have been adopted become obsessed with a desire to know about or meet their birth parents. Organizations have sprung up to help people in these searches.

How often when we see a product do we ask, I wonder who made that or who built it? Somehow, we think if we can determine the origin of someone or something, we have gathered important information. These answers are really part of discovering how the world works and, in some cases, discovering something about whom we are.

The point is creation is about origins. This thirsty curiosity seems to be in all of us. Where did mankind come from? What was the beginning of the things we see? How did it all happen? That drive was placed in us by our Creator to give us a hunger to move to find Him.

The answer to the question of where did all this around me come from and where did I come from is God. *"In the beginning God..."* (Genesis 1:1). Now let's explore what idolatry looks like in our current days. What could some of the idols be? Let's consider particularly those idols that explicitly deny God as the Creator.

A major suspect is the idol of science. Most specifically we will look at the part of science known as evolution because evolution is about origin. The basic tenets of this idol are the notion that not only did God not create the world and all that is in it, but there was never any divine involvement in the origin of life and the world. The world and life have come into being by a series of chemical or mechanical events.

What is seen today in the world and in life is the product of gradual changes over a long period of time. Since probability is involved in calculating these gradual changes, a great deal of time is needed to allow for these changes that are involved in the process. It is good to pause and remember that when observing this kind of thinking, it is coming from a mind that is foolish and confused and that has trivialized itself and thinks it knows it all.

Brazenly the theorists who are the priests of this idol assign millions of years of time for these changes, and in some cases even attribute billions of years. A basic tenet of elementary science is in order to be a scientific fact, it must be observable and measurable and also the fact must be able to be reproduced. None of the foundational concepts of evolution can pass muster for this standard.

A recent article explained the great dilemma scientists are facing because they have discovered that there are issues with the "Big Bang" theory that has been so popular as an explanation for the origin of the earth. Here is an excerpt:

> The most elite scientists in the world are still struggling to find why exactly our universe didn't destroy itself as soon as it came into existence. That's what science says should have happened—but it clearly hasn't, since you're here reading this, as far as we know.
>
> At the beginning of the universe, according to the standard model, there were equal amounts of matter and anti-matter. The trouble with that is that they would each have annihilated each other, leaving none of the matter that surrounds us today.
>
> Researchers have been frantically looking for some difference between matter and anti-matter that could explain why the universe is still around. But they have tried a range of different possibilities—that they have different mass, electric charge, or something else—but have found no difference (https://hotair.com/archives/2017/10/25/scientists-finally-admit-universe-shouldntexist/?utm_source=hadaily&utm_ medium=email&utm_campaign=nl).

The Idol

What has happened is people have denied creation, and the creator and the idol they have created is science—specifically evolution.

When People Believe Not-Truth

Those who choose to deny God as the Creator have turned to their vain imaginations and professed themselves to be wise. With vain imaginations a person can go anywhere in their thinking.

Imagination does not require evidence and is by itself beyond what is real. Imagination is a kind of a creation. With imagination the mind can go anywhere. Sometimes children have imaginary friends. Usually family members just humor the child and go along with their imaginations. The imaginary friend usually has a name and many qualities and characteristics. Hopefully, a time will come when the child realizes that the friend is not real.

Eugene Peterson in his book, *Christ Plays in Ten Thousand Places*, cites some insights from G. K. Chesterton that illustrate the operation of vain imaginations.

> G. K. Chesterton once said that that there are two kinds of people in the world: When trees are waving wildly in the wind, one group of people thinks that it is the wind that moves the trees; the other group of people thinks that the motion of the trees create the wind. The former view was the one held by most of humankind through most of the centuries; it was only in recent years, Chesterton said, that a new breed of people emerged who blandly hold that it is the movement of the trees that creates the wind. The consensus had always been that the invisible is behind and gives energy to the visible; Chesterton in his work as a journalist, closely observing and commenting on people and events, reported with alarm that the broad consensus had fallen apart and that a modern majority naively assumes that what they see and hear and touch is basic reality and generates whatever people come up with that cannot be verified with the senses. They think that the visible accounts for the invisible (p. 20-21).

The vain imaginations of the last century and a half have gone to evolution as the explanation of origins. Today many accept the theory of evolution as a scientific fact. It is taught in our schools and accepted in the general culture. Since imagination is without limits, explanation can include amazing proportions. Small fragments of fossilized bones are declared to be great evidence of prehistoric animals or humans. Gigantic declarations are made about the relationship between different animals. All of this is declared to be scientific.

Once again, we can see that beliefs drive practice. They are believing that the idol, science, is the truth, and this drives the practice of excluding God's creation as an explanation for what is observed and exists.

Looking closer at the evolutionary conceptualization of origins, we see a pattern. As they look backward toward origins, they see all life forms to have originated with one common life cell. There is considerable conjecture about how this first accident occurred that resulted in life. Perhaps lightning struck a mineral-rich scum pond and presto this first cell emerged. They conclude that all life forms have a common ancestor—this single cell. Then they surmise that over long periods of time, this cell evolved into a more complex life forms and divergence began to happen. Through occasional mutations, the life form takes on a different shape and different characteristics.

The uniqueness of each life form is further defined by the adaption they make that allows them to survive in their environment. A recognized principle is "survival of the fittest." Survival becomes the major theme of this thinking. The ultimate goal of each life form is to survive because failure to survive equates to failure to exist. For all these gradual changes to occur and all the necessary adapting for survival necessitates great periods of time i.e. millions and millions of years. Once again, we can see that these beliefs drive practice. Believing the evolution basis for a definition for origins drives the practice of creating outlandish explanations for beginnings.

Does scripture give a hint that such thinking might occur? In a prophetic way we can see this was foretold by Peter.

First off, you need to know that in the last days, mockers are going to have a heyday. Reducing everything to the level of their puny feelings, they'll mock, "So what's happened to the promise of his Coming? Our ancestors are dead and buried, and everything's going on just as it has from the first day of creation. Nothing's changed."

They conveniently forget that long ago all the galaxies and this very planet were brought into existence out of watery chaos by God's word. Then God's word brought the chaos back in a flood that destroyed the world. The current galaxies and earth are fuel for the final fire. God is poised, ready to speak his word again, ready to give the signal for the judgment and destruction of the desecrating skeptics (II Peter 3:3-5 The Message).

An assumption in evolutionary theory is that of a continuum. They view a timeline of ongoing increments without interruption. Peter points out that there are major and catastrophic events that result in major and sudden changes. Peter specifically refers to the flood of Noah. We cannot conceptualize periods of time of millions of years. And what is postulated to have occurred during those periods is unknowable.

The basic tenets of their theory are not supported by basic logic. Yet these tenets are boldly taught as facts, and what is observed in the environment (called nature) and life is explained and interpreted based on these tenets. The statements of explanation that defy logic are just blown over, and people are expected to accept them as fact. The followers of the idol of evolution are forced to accept the tenets' accuracy by faith.

Survival

Looking closer at the central premise of survival in evolutionary thinking, we see that an element of that is the function of reproduction. This is part of survival of the species. There needs to be a next generation for the gradual changes to occur. A presupposition of this thinking is that this change process is always moving from a lower level of complexity to a higher level of complexity. Even though the life forms are organized into categories based on similarities and sorted into families with the assumption of common ancestors, each life form is an isolated individual.

Interestingly, the human being is considered to be the highest order of life form and abides in the animal family, specifically a group called homo sapiens. The status of the most highly developed has to do with brain size and the capacity for speech. However, this advanced capacity does not make human beings any more valuable among life forms in this pattern of thinking.

A kind of logic exists within this system of thinking that says if all life forms are the product of time and chance and a natural progression of the survival of the fittest, then human beings are just one of the many with no unique and special value. Once again, we can see that these beliefs drive practice. Believing the evolutionary basis for a definition of human life drives the practice of discounting the value of human beings.

When we look at the concept of similarities being the result of a common ancestor, which fits the evolutionist presuppositions, could there be another simpler explanation? The creationist response would say obviously the similarities are the product of a common designer or Creator.

When an art expert is consulted to identify works of art, whether paintings or sculpture, they use evidence of similarities to determine a common artist. These experts can write volumes about fine details and distinctive characteristics of an individual artist. When a famous architect's work is being analyzed, the distinctive characteristics of the architect's work are explained. In both of these examples, the obvious conclusion is these works contain similarities because they are the result of a common creator.

More Consequences

Let's look specifically at the practice of abortion, which has become so common in today's society. If a woman believes that she is a product of time and chance and only one of many co-equal life forms, she has a trivialized view of herself. Also, personal survival is a primary goal. Personal survival is assured by paying attention to safety, comfort, and convenience. After all each person gets one life here on earth and then after that, there is cessation of existence.

Although an element of survival is reproduction, it is not primary. Mysteriously, it can be observed that all life forms, plant or animal, have some drive to reproduce. The thinking for the evolutionary woman is that it is their choice about participation in reproduction. After all, if she experiences an unwanted pregnancy, she can evaluate how this impacts her comfort, convenience, or wishes as it relates to her view of her survival. She can choose to terminate the pregnancy.

To do this, she can lean on her definition of life forms drawn from her evolutionary thinking. Since she is an isolated individual who is part of a category of life forms that is part of a pattern of ever evolving species, such is true of other life forms including her baby. To terminate another life, the unborn baby, simply becomes a function of an act of personal survival.

Here is a quote from an abortion activist:
> All life is not equal. That's a difficult thing for liberals like me to talk about, lest we wind up looking like death-panel-loving, kill-your-grandma-and-your-precious-baby storm troopers. Yet a fetus can be a human life without having the same rights as the woman in whose body it resides. She's the boss. Her life and what is right for her circumstances and her health should automatically trump the rights of the non-autonomous entity inside of her. Always.

However, this act of termination creates some internal conflict because it is not universally accepted by all of society. There are many fellow human beings who do not believe the same way. The abortion seeker and the abortion activist create a pattern of thinking to justify terminating a pregnancy. A common position is that the unborn baby is part of the woman's body, and she has the right to do with her body as she chooses.

Another position is that the unborn baby is not a human being before it is born. The unborn baby is just a mass of cells and available to be chemically or mechanically removed from the mother's uterus. The sad thing is this pattern of thinking is not inconsistent with the thinking of the idol of evolution. Remember the prime objective is survival of the mother as experienced by her comfort, convenience, and desires.

Once again, we can see that these beliefs drive practice. Believing the evolution basis for a definition of an unborn baby the mother is driven to the practice of abortion.

Chapter 9

Spiraling Down

Little children, keep yourselves from idols. Amen (I John 5:21).

What was the result of turning to idols? What did God do? Looking on in Romans 1, we will see a long and sad list of what happens.

> *Wherefore God also gave them up to uncleanness through the lust of their own hearts, to dishonor their own bodies between themselves: Who changed the truth of God into a lie, and worshipped and served the creature more than the Creator, who is blessed forever. Amen. For this cause God gave them up unto vile affections: for even their women did change the natural use into that which is against nature: And likewise the men, leaving the natural use of a woman, burned in their lust one toward another; men with men working that which is unseemly, and receiving in themselves that recompense of their error which was meet. And even as they did not like to retain God in their knowledge, God gave them over to a reprobate mind, to do those things which are not convenient; Being filled with all unrighteousness, fornication, wickedness, covetousness, maliciousness, full of envy, murder, debate, deceit, malignity; whispers, backbiters, haters of God, despiteful, proud, boasters, inventers of evil things, disobedient to parents, without understanding, covenantbreakers, without nat-*

ural affection, implacable, unmerciful: who knowing the judgment of God, that they which commit such things are worthy of death, not only do the same, but have pleasure in them that do them (Romans 1:24-32).

This is a long passage, the list of unrighteousness is very long, and how we would rate the seriousness of the different items in the list would vary. But God has seen fit to include them in the list. Let's look at God's specific actions and remember this is all in response to personal act of individuals of denying God as creator and replacing Him with an idol or idols. *God also gave them up to… God gave them up unto… God gave them over to….*

Let's look at what is happening to the thinking of man. *Who changed the truth of God into a lie… worshipped and served the creature more than the Creator… changed the truth of God into a lie… who knowing the judgment of God… that they which commit such things are worthy of death… have pleasure in them that do them….*

We see the tragic results of the person who has rejected God as creator as their foolish mind becomes darkened, they choose in a state of thinking that they know it all, and they turn to idols. We see God's response in giving them up and turning them over, resulting in God's judgment in their current lives. In spite of knowing that this is God's judgment, they continue on in their ways.

Notice in this long list of unrighteous acts that all of them result in harm or hurt to the person committing the acts and often in harm or hurt to others. This is not the end of the story because the Bible goes on to record how people did and have turned from their idols to God the Creator. It records how their lives changed. It records how they found a vital, satisfying, and meaningful relationship with God.

Before we look more closely at the list of sinful behaviors from this chapter, let's look at an observation by Tozer: "When men no longer fear God, they transgress His laws without hesitation. The fear of consequences is no deterrent when the fear of God is gone" (p. 77).

At this point it becomes helpful to look back at the list of behaviors that are the result of choosing to not embrace God as creator or to identify all life forms and the earth's systems as a product of His creation. Let's look at abortion once again and specifically, that the woman does not recognize herself as a created being. What do we see?

First of all, we see that they *worshipped and served the creature more than the Creator.* The individual person has become the most important thing in their world. *Fornication* is involved because the woman became pregnant. And although sometimes the pregnancy that is terminated resulted from the relationship between a husband and wife, most often that is not the case. *Murder* has occurred, and it is first degree murder because the life of the baby is taken with deliberate foreknowledge and planning.

Also, there are witnesses because the abortionists and assistants are present during the killing procedure and are actually accomplices. Another behavior from the list is *unmerciful.* The life of a defenseless baby is taken. The aborting mother is *without natural affection.* Throughout the world and throughout history, the power and depth of a mother's love for her offspring is well known and acclaimed. Just how strong is the natural affection of a mother for her child? Let's look at scripture to see a situation where God is seeking to demonstrate the strength and intensity of His commitment to us. Look at the contrast He draws.

> *Can a mother forget her sucking child, that she should not have compassion on the son of her womb? Yea, they may forget, yet will I not forget thee* (Isaiah 49:15).

In addition, we can wonder at those who are so supportive of the abortion movement and who so vehemently advocate abortions. This group includes males who will never be pregnant and females who may never experience an unwanted pregnancy. They identify themselves as members of the "choice" movement. This is a name that is meant to be deceiving and avoids the term "abortion."

It is obvious that self-interest would be driving members of the abortion industry because of their desire for financial gain. However, we wonder about others who are either activists or are simply supporters. What is their thinking? Previously, we have looked at the kind of thinking that comes from believing in the evolutionary idol's explanation of origins and life. The supporters are thinking this way. But why are the activists so angry and driven?

Once again, remember the state of mind of those who have rejected the thinking of God as creator and mankind as created beings. Remember this is a product of a foolish and confused mind that has trivialized itself and thinks it knows it all. A characteristic of people who think they know it all is to be overbearing, defensive, and dogmatic.

In summary, the result of denying God as Creator results in a reprobate mind that trivializes oneself and others. The aborting mother has trivialized herself and her baby. She finds security in her decision because she believes that she knows it all.

It is only natural for it to follow that the behaviors in the list that occurs as a result of God giving them over shows up in the act of abortion. It is the sad, sad conclusion that the thinking that supports and surrounds the idol of evolutionary thinking provides the atmosphere that supports the brutal act of abortion.

Once again, we can see that these beliefs drive practice. We have seen how this long list of wrong beliefs drives many wrong practices.

Reprobate Mind

What are some of the implications of the vain imaginations denying God as the Creator? A basic concept is that what is created is the property of the Creator. Most countries have patent and copyright laws to protect the property of the person who did the creating. If God created us, we are His property.

However, if people do not believe that God created them, then they are not God's property; and if they are not God's property, they become free moral agents. They belong only to themselves and have no responsibility to anyone but themselves. There is no accountability to a higher power because they are the higher power. If mankind is simply the product of time and chance, then a person is not accountable to anyone.

This person has lost the dignity of being created in the image of God and has become their own god. The value of life has been reduced because mankind is only a highly evolved animal. With this belief it becomes possible to abort an unborn baby because it is just an animal. The vain imagination can even claim the fetus is not even a human before it is born. This loss of respect for human life can be extended to other people. Euthanasia becomes acceptable for part of the evolutionary theory includes the survival of the fittest.

Once again, we can see that these beliefs drive practice. Believing that a person is not a created being that belongs to God and therefore that person belongs to themselves drives a practice of being unaccountable except to one's own self.

Remember acknowledging God as Creator is the foundational thinking required to understand the current world and what has happened historically. On a personal level acknowledging God as Creator is the foundational thinking needed to develop a personal relationship with God. The scripture states that when people knew God perfectly well but refused to honor Him as God, they trivialized themselves.

What could trivializing yourself mean? When anything or anyone is trivialized, their value is diminished. The cool phrase these days is "dissed." How can that be? The clear message from the creation story is that God considers mankind a highly valued creature. Mankind is a special creation that has been created in the image of God and has the role of having dominion over the rest of creation.

This truth makes each individual created by God very special and very valuable and should not be trivialized. However, when a person has chosen to disregard or deny the fact they are a special and valued creation of God, they have just trivialized themselves. This is a very sad thing. We grieve when we are around someone or witness someone showing what we call "low self-esteem" or what we call having a "poor self-image." They are trivializing themselves.

Once again, we can see that these beliefs drive practice. Believing that you are not a special and valued creation of God drives the practice of trivializing yourself.

Now watch what happens. They take their trivialized self into silliness and confusion so that there is neither sense nor direction in their lives, and they become directionless. How sad. They do what people often do. They begin to compensate by pretending to know it all but misunderstand life. Their thinking is all messed up. Remember the warning: be careful what you think.

Let's look further to see what happens next.

> *And changed the glory of the uncorruptible God into an image made like corruptible man, and to birds, and four-footed beasts and creeping things* (Romans 1:23).

Idols Again

In their confusion following denying God as their Creator, they made idols. With their own hands they created images and declared that the image that they had just created had made them. Then they bowed down and worshiped it. These images are really a product of an idea that involves supernatural powers and super knowledge attributed to the idol. The idol becomes a symbol of the idea or thinking.

The idol is the visible representative of this thinking. The idol worshiper knows about the power attributed to the idol that it is just another rock or chunk of wood or a piece of metal. This has been going on throughout the history of man and is still going on today. How foolish is that? But remember this is a product of a foolish and confused mind that has trivialized itself and thinks it knows it all.

Eugene Peterson explains the attractiveness of creating idols for those who have denied the Creator and are operating with their vain imaginations and thinking themselves to be wise.

Idols are non-gods and as such are much more congenial to us than God, for we not only have pleasure of making them, using our wonderful imaginations and skills in creative ways, but also of controlling them. They are gods with all of the God taken out so that we can continue to be our own gods. There are innumerable ways in which we can make idols for ourselves. The possibilities are endless, ranging from the skies above to the earth around us to the sea beneath us. It is no wonder that idol-making and idol-worshiping have always been the most popular religious game in town (*Christ Plays in Ten Thousand Places*, p. 254).

Let's pause here and remind ourselves of the first of the Ten Commandments.

Thou shalt have none other gods before me. Thou shalt not make thee any graven image, or any likeness of anything that is in heaven above, or that is in the earth beneath, or that is in the waters beneath the earth: Thou shalt not bow down thyself unto them, nor serve them: for I the Lord thy God am a jealous God, visiting the iniquity of the fathers upon the children unto the third and fourth generations of them that hate me. And shewing mercy unto thousands of them that love me and keep my commandments (Deuteronomy 5: 7-10).

An idol is any object, person, concept, theory, philosophy, or dogma that a person puts in the place of God. This is why the thinking that acknowledges God as Creator is so important.

There is a principle that is generally true: "going before—following after." This a general concept that works for understanding sequences. It works for designing flow charts. It works for following a map. It works for following a recipe. It works here: deny God as Creator, and the confused thinking that believes it knows it all will create an idol to replace God as Creator. Denying God (going before) —creating idols (following after).

Spiraling Down

In *Knowledge of the Holy*, Tozer, in discussing the result of denying God as creator, says:

> Then followed the worship of idols fashioned after the likeness of men and birds and beasts and creeping things. But this series of degrading acts began in the mind. Wrong ideas about God are not only the fountain from which polluted water of idolatry flow; they are themselves idolatrous. The idolater simply imagines things about God and acts as if they were true.
>
> Perverted notions about God soon rot the religion in which they appear. The long career of Israel demonstrates this clearly enough, and the history of the Church confirms it (p. 12).

Once again, we can see that these beliefs drive practice. The belief of denying God as Creator and the confused thinking that believes it knows it all will drive the practice of creating an idol to replace God as Creator. We have been illustrating how the principle of belief drives practice works when beliefs are not based on truth, specifically denial of God as Creator.

This is part of the *"mystery of iniquity that is already working"* (I Thessalonians 2:7). This is clearly a negative example, but it also vividly demonstrates how the validity of the principle of belief drives practice. Now I want to turn to the positive and how the principle of belief drives practice works in the mystery of godliness.

Let's once again contrast the wonder of God's creation with the attitudes that permeate around the idol of science. In his *Knowledge of the Holy*, Tozer quotes Carlyle:

> "It is not by our superior insight that we escape a satiety of wonder," says Carlyle, "it is by our superior levity, our inattention, our want of insight. It is by not thinking that we cease

to wonder at it...We call that fire of the blackened thundercloud 'electricity' and lecture learnedly about it, and grind the like of it out of glass and silk: but what is it? Whence comes it? Science has done much for us; but it is poor science that would hide from us the great deed sacred infinitude of Nescience, whither we can never penetrate, on which all science swims as a mere superficial film. This world, after all our science and sciences is still a miracle; wonderful, inscrutable, magical and more, to whosoever will think of it."

These penetrating, almost prophetic, words were written more than a century ago, but not all the breath-taking advances of science and technology since that time have invalidated one word or rendered obsolete as much as one period or comma. Still we do not know. We save face by repeating frivolously the popular jargon of science. We harness the mighty energy that rushes through the world; we subject it to finger tip control in our cars and kitchens; we make it to work for us like Aladdin's jinn, but still we do not know what it is. Secularism, materialism, and the intrusive presence of *things* have put out the light of our souls and turned us into zombies. We cover our deep ignorance with words, but we are ashamed to wonder, we are afraid to whisper "mystery" (page 26).

People who base their belief system about who they are and how the world works on a denial of God as Creator are building their house on the sand. You can see that belief in creation is absolutely foundational.

> *And every one that heareth these sayings of mine, and doeth them not, shall be likened unto a foolish man, which built his house upon the sand: And the rain descended, and the floods came, and the winds blew, and beat upon that house; and it fell: and great was the fall of it* (Matthew 7:26-27).

Spiraling Down

This has been a heavy and dark chapter, and we will move on to more positive applications, but I think it is important and sobering to look at the consequences of believing **not truth**. Perhaps these solemn considerations provide a serious motivation to strength our resolve to seek **truth** and believe it.

Chapter 10

Truth and Life

> There are some truths that God will make simple. The only thing God makes plain in the Bible is the way to salvation and sanctification, after that our understanding depends on our walking in the light (Oswald Chambers in *My Utmost for His Highest*).

In John 14, Jesus stated that He was the way, the truth, and the life. We have discussed how He was the way and explored some about how He is the truth, and now we want to look at how He is the life.

First, let's briefly discuss physical life, which is something that is visible. Physical life's counterpart is physical death. Life begins at conception and ends with the termination of body functions. At conception all of sudden there is life that was not there before the instant of conception.

At physical death there is a time when life is no longer there. Life was there, however feeble, and then it was no longer there. Many of us have witnessed the passing from life to death. It may have been with the passing of a person or an animal. We have certainly seen dramatizations of the arrival of death in movies or on television. Both life and death have a moment of their appearance.

This is true of all of God's creation. In God's creative planning, He instituted the process of reproduction to increase and multiply. In Genesis, we see that the creation was to reproduce *"after its kind."* We see the reproduction occurring in all plants and animals.

For some of creation, the production involves fertilization and conception. For some of creation, it involves germination of seeds. There also other interesting ways of reproducing after its kind that God has included in His creation. The point is there is a time when life begins for all of God's living creation.

Conversely, there is a time when death occurs. Recently we had a killing frost. My squash plants and flowers are dead. They were alive and well when I went to bed, and they were dead when I woke up the next morning. Most of us have had beloved pets who grew old and died or perhaps were killed by a predator or in an accident. One day they were alive, and the next day they were dead. This is the reality of the current age.

Our present and temporary bodies are in the process of wearing out. Over time, strength and energy decline. Work and disease begin to take their toll. Eventually, we too will die. God knows the time for each one of us. We read that our days are numbered, and it is appointed unto man once to die. This is the reality of physical life and physical death. Also, this is not what Jesus was talking about when He said He was life.

Another way we think about life has to do with our circumstance and conditions. Sometimes we are thinking about how our life is currently. We ask, "How is your life?" or "How is life treating you?" We want to know if the daily happenings in a person's life are going well.

When I apply that question to myself today, I must say that my life is going well. The Lord has provided a wonderful best friend of a wife, and we dearly love each other. He has provided a comfortable home and all necessary provision for each day. For senior citizens, we generally enjoy satisfactory health, even though we do have our daily medications and routine doctor appointments. We enjoy our daily routines that include activities that seem to match our strength levels. We enjoy our neighbors, friends and relatives. However, we can also think of life as the total span of years on this earth in these physical bodies with all the challenges, trials, losses, opportunities, disasters, blessings, events, etc.

As a senior citizen, I have many years to review and I must say that I have experienced the entire list seen in the previous sentence. With the advantage of perspective, I can identify God's hand all along the way. This does not mean I understand everything that has happened and certainly doesn't mean I don't wish some things had not happened. But God is good and I trust His purposes. This description of life is not what Jesus meant when He said that He was the life.

When Jesus said He was the life, He was talking about the life of God. Remember how the Spirit of God comes to dwell in the born-again believer? The very life of God is in each believer in Christ. Often this life is referred to as eternal life or everlasting life. This is almost too much to grasp. Certainly, this is part of *"other"* and *"beyond."*

> *For God so loved the world, that He gave His only begotten son, that whosoever believeth in Him should not perish, but have everlasting life* (John 3:16).
>
> *I am come that might have life, and they might have it more abundantly* (John 10:10).

Truth and Life

This life that Jesus gives is everlasting and abundant. This is the life that is working in the believer for the transformational change with a renewed mind into the godliness that is our mystery. Bit by bit we are identifying clues and gaining insight and understanding into the mystery of godliness!

Chapter 11

Transforming into Godliness

> Sanctification means an intense concentration on God's point of view—every power of spirit, soul and body chained and kept for God's purpose only (Oswald Chambers).

Now let's explore further how our principle of belief drives practice works out in our transformation into godliness. Since this is a dynamic principle, it will automatically happen. That is if the belief is based on truth it will automatically drive the practice (words, thoughts, and deeds) to create godliness.

Said another way, the right belief will produce the right practice, or a belief based on God's truth will produce a godly practice. The proper input will produce the proper output. The individual's role in the principle's operation is the choice or decision about what to believe.

Let's pause for a moment and think about this further. Are there concepts in scripture that would support what appears to be a passive role for the believer? One could argue that choosing what to believe is hardly passive, but the focus is now on the automatic process of the principle.

Remember the illustration that Jesus gave us of the vine and branches in which He is the vine and we are the branches? The branches receive their life and substance from the vine. The branches are entirely dependent on the vine for life. If the branches were to be cut off, they would no longer be living.

> *Abide in me, and I in you. As the branch cannot bear fruit of itself, except it abide in the vine, no more can ye, except ye abide in me. I am the vine, ye are the branches: He that abideth in me, and I in him, the same bringeth forth much fruit for without Me you can do nothing* (John 15:4-5).

The life force that is at play in our belief drives practice principle is that the very life of God that is present in the believer takes the belief in God's truth and yields godly practice (much fruit).

> *If ye keep my commandments, ye shall abide in my love, even as I have kept my Father's commandments, and abide in His love* (John 15:10).

Here we see a link between love and obedience and the commandments as God's statements of truth.

In Hebrews 4:3,9-10, we read,

> *For we which have believed do enter into rest...There remaineth therefore a rest to the people of God. For he that has entered into his rest, he also has that ceased from his own works, as God did from His.*

The need for effort for the believer is past because God has completed His work of our salvation. These passages in Hebrews go on to expound the value of the scriptures in directing believers into the truth.

Abiding and resting seem so passive. It seems like the believer should be doing something. Before we look into what the believer should be doing, let's look a little more at abiding and resting.

But the fruit of the Spirit is love, joy, peace, longsuffering, gentleness, goodness, faith, meekness, temperance: against such there is no law (Galatians 5:22).

For the fruit of the Spirit is in all goodness and righteousness and truth, proving what is acceptable unto the Lord (Romans 5:9-10).

Now we know what the fruit looks like. What a nice list! Notice there is no law against them. Can you think of a law against loving? Can you think of a law against gentleness? Let's take a moment and tie this back in with the citizens of the Kingdom of God. Harold St. John, who was a missionary and Bible teacher from England, speaking of believers' behavior spoke of court manners. I like this concept and I am sure he is referring back to proper and polite behavior and protocols to be practiced in the courts of the royalty and aristocracy.

Those of us from the colonies may not lay much stock in such goings on, but polite and proper behavior is still important. We don't like rudeness. I think the list of fruit of the Spirit fit nicely into good manners worthy of proper behavior in the Kingdom of God. It has been pointed out that the scripture says fruit singular not fruits plural. The fruit of the Spirit is a package deal. The existence of fruit of the Spirit gives an idea of what godliness looks like.

Jerry Bridges in his book, *The Practice of Godliness*, states:
> Some of the traits of godly character appear to blend together much as different shades of thread in a garment or colors in a rainbow. Patience for example, closely resembles joy and peace in its effect upon our lives (p. 203).

James gives insight in "court manners":

> *But the wisdom that is from above is first pure, then peaceable, gentle, and easy to be entreated, full of mercy and good fruits, without partiality, and without hypocrisy. And the fruit of righteousness is sown in peace of them that make peace* (James 3:17-18).

The Word of God

We still need to look into what a believer is supposed to do. Going back and reviewing our principle of belief drives practice, let's dive into belief. We have already suggested that in the path to godliness it is important that the belief be based on truth. We noted that Jesus said He is the truth. We also distinguished between what is **truth** and **not-truth**. We also established that faith is just believing. *"The just shall live by faith"* (Romans 1:17). Let's settle on the proposition that the path to godliness is based on believing the truth. Let's also declare that truth is to be found in the Word of God.

> *For the word of God is quick, and powerful, and sharper than any two edged sword, piercing even to the dividing asunder of soul and spirit, and the joints and marrow, and is a discerner of the thoughts and intents of the heart* (Hebrews 4:12).

> *Study to shew thyself approved unto God, a workman that needeth not be ashamed, rightly dividing the word of truth* (II Timothy 2:15).

> *All scripture is given by inspiration of God, and is profitable for doctrine, for reproof, for correction, for instruction in righteousness: That the man of God may be perfect, thoroughly furnished unto all good works* (II Timothy 3:16-17).

We have a more sure word of prophecy; whereunto ye do well that ye take heed, as unto a light that shineth in a dark place, until the day star rise in your hearts: Knowing this first, that no prophecy of the scripture is of any private interpretation. For the prophecy came not in old time by the will of man: but holy men of God spake as they were moved by the Holy Ghost (II Peter 1:19-21)

Clearly the truth that is to be believed is found in the word of God. So, if the believer is to know the truth they must be reading the word of God. That sounds pretty simple! The instructions found in the scriptures tell us what to do and what not to do. There is also instruction about how to handle different situations with others and matters of personal stewardship of God's provisions and creation.

In the Bible we also learn about who God is, what He has done, and much about what He is going to do. The believer's job is to know it. If you are going to believe the truth, you must know the truth. This is all straightforward and clear.

Let's think a little more about believing the truth. Think in terms of quantity of truth. The straightforward results of our formula—believing the truth drives godly practice—is logically the more truth believed, the more godly practice. We have established that the truth is found in the scriptures, therefore it follows that the better a believer knows the scriptures, the more truthful data they have to believe. Now it is easy to see that here is a process: more in—more out, more truth—more practice.

Thy word have I hid in mine heart, that I might not sin against thee (Psalms 119:11).

Not so fast! Remember what we learned about the self-system? Let's review. We start out as babies who are born sinners; we have a sin nature as a result of the fall. We begin to answer the question who am I as an individual and progress on to figuring out how things work in the world. Who I am and how the world works are mysteries to each of us that we spend our whole life seeking to solve. The wonderful news is there are answers, and they are found in the truth. God is in the business of guiding us into these answers.

When we become believers, we seek answers to the question who am I as a child of God in the Kingdom of God. We also begin to figure out how things work in God's family in the Kingdom of God. In every case, on our pursuit to become godly as part of the mystery of godliness, we want our beliefs to be based on the truth. For the most part we do not naturally know the truth; we have to learn it.

We can learn it by being taught the truth or by reading the truth from the scriptures. Here is the bummer. We are exposed to a lot of **not-truth**. The Lord says:

> *For my thoughts are not your thoughts, neither are your ways my ways, saith the Lord. For as the heavens are higher than the earth, so are my ways higher than your ways, and my thoughts than your thoughts* (Isaiah 55:8-9).

It is good to remember that the transformation is a developmental process. Becoming godly is a progression. Believers move to maturity.

Learning

Now what we learned about how the brain operates further complicates the process even though that knowledge is helpful. We must learn the truth. Let's review the brain's operation. Remember the earlier illustration about the sick ewe and the veterinarian? Through our senses multiple inputs come into our sensory memory where the inputs are sorted, and some move on to the working memory. After a short stay in working memory, some of the inputs are moved to the permanent memory. There may also be some interaction in which stored inputs in the permanent memory are retrieved and interact with the new input in the working memory.

All these processes happen very quickly, often automatically, and usually we are unaware of them. The whole process is something to be marveled at as a product of being a wonderful creation. All of this can go on in each of our heads without our ever knowing about the process. The net effect is that learning takes place.

Let's look more closely at learning. Any and all learning results in change. When you and I learn some bit of knowledge or a new skill, we are changed. The person we were before the learning experience is not the same person we are after the learning experience. What's more we will never again be the person we were before the learning experience.

The change may be very small and probably is small. Usually we will not be aware of the change. However, sometimes the change is significant, and we are very aware of it. We often call the big change moment an "ah ha" moment.

Let me illustrate with a very mundane example. Recently in a conversation with my brother-in-law, he was telling me about how his brother had to pay $800 to get his vehicle repaired. The problem resulted from his brother's practice of filling his gas tank to the brim. After the gas valve automatically shut off, he would keep squeezing the lever on the nozzle until the gas tank was completely full.

This was an "ah ha" moment for me. I had just learned something that I didn't know before ,and it was relevant because through the years I had often practiced what my brother-in-law's brother was doing. Sometimes I would do it just to round off the amount I had to pay to the nearest dollar, and sometimes I would do it because I thought I had a good price on the gasoline. Needless to say, because of what I learned I now quit pumping gas when the automatic valve on the nozzle shuts off. I spread my new knowledge by telling my wife.

I recently went one step farther when standing next to a friend while he was filling his gas tank, and he began to keep squeezing the lever on the nozzle after it had automatically shut off. I proceeded to share my knowledge with him. I was changed by this new knowledge, and my friend was changed by this new knowledge. I have no idea if he will change his practice when filling a gas tank but he might.

The point is we are changed by what we learn. Here is another illustration. For years in many different settings, I have taught the principle: "Once you see something, you cannot not see it." Let me explain. Sometime after our house was built, it settled. This is not unusual and is to be expected. The settling was not a structural problem or a matter of concern. One of the effects was a few small cracks appeared in the dry wall. One crack was located at the peak of the cathedral ceiling on the north and south walls of the house. It is a small crack.

I have no idea how long the crack had been there before I happened to notice it one day. However, since I have noticed it, I cannot look at that part of the house without seeing that crack. Another crack has appeared in one corner of a bedroom. The same scenario has occurred.

Learning is progressive and the change that we experience is progressive. Progressive change is transformational. The *"renewing of our minds"* process resulting in our being transformed into the image of Christ is progressive. The act of learning accumulates into a store of knowledge. I think we can assume that this store of knowledge resides in our permanent memory. This storehouse is where our beliefs reside.

As life plays out on a daily basis, our wonderful brains will access this storehouse to retrieve our beliefs. These beliefs will then drive our practice. Over time we acquire these beliefs, and the beliefs that are based on the truth will move us in the direction of godliness.

Interestingly, most of those beliefs will be linked to providing information on our self-system—who we are or how things work. The illustration about filling a gas tank relates to how things work. The illustration is mundane and it may be a stretch to see how it relates to godliness. However, I can think of some ways.

First of all, it relates to good stewardship of what the Lord has provided: wise care of vehicles. Second, it was kind of my brother-in-law to give me the information. Third, it was kind of me to pass my new knowledge on to my wife and friend. All of these are godly behaviors.

We have examined how learning leads to change and that often we are not aware of the change, or it is difficult to detect. Also, usually it is not relevant that we be aware of the change. Let's take the time to look more closely at the change using a familiar story, the story of the sick ewe and the veterinarian. You remember that we used this story to very exhaustively explore how the three stages of memory played out during this episode.

So now let's speculate on the learning that may have happened. Did my wife and I learn about symptoms of a sick ewe? No, we already knew that. Did our veterinarian learn about diagnosing and treating the sick ewe? No, he already knew that. One of the things my wife and I learned was that our observations about the ewe's behavior were valid. Our concern was confirmed. We also learned that our decision to call the veterinarian and our belief in his ability were valid. This decision was confirmed. We learned that we could trust our experience, and we were changed because we have increased confidence in our capacity to respond to similar issues in the future.

In a similar way the veterinarian had his diagnosis and treatment responses confirmed. He reaffirmed his knowledge and skill base so that he was changed to become even more confident in his ability to practice veterinary medicine. I am sure that not one of three of us spent any energy analyzing our learning and the way we were changed, but nevertheless it happened. These dynamics happen many times every day in everyone's life. It is part of the marvelous way we were created.

With all this exploration of our brain and memory processes, you are probably wondering where thinking fits into the principle, belief drives practice. Earlier we mentioned that we think mainly in words. Where do words come from? In *Knowledge of the Holy*, Tozer commented:

> Thoughts and speech are God's gifts to creatures made in His image; they are intimately associated with Him and impossible apart from Him. It is highly significant that the first word was the Word: *And the Word was with God, and the Word was God."* We may speak because God spoke. In Him word and idea are indivisible (page 20).

We also know that people think much faster than they can talk or read. We can also think about other things while doing something different than what we are thinking about. Amazingly we can be thinking about something different than the content of something we are reading or when someone else is speaking to us.

Generally, this is a good thing. Our thinking may be analyzing or evaluating what is being input through what we see or hear. When you stop to think about it, we spend a lot of our waking time thinking. Who knows what thinking is involved in our sleep time dreams? Thankfully, that is not to be considered here.

Decisions

First let's look at how thinking relates to believing. We talked about a decision-making process involved in our determination of a belief. Often, we are not aware of the decision process but never the less it is there. We use thinking to help in coming to a determination of what is a belief.

As mentioned earlier, this happens in our self-system—who am I and how things work. We also have looked at the alignment between a belief and the truth. Believers who desire to become godly will be committed to having their beliefs aligned with the truth. Our thinking will rely on our knowledge. This is a connection with learning. Obviously, we have learned our knowledge. What is the source of that knowledge? Where did we learn it?

We have stressed the reliability of the word of God as a source of the truth. But it is important to acknowledge that another valuable source of knowledge and place of learning is the Bible based teaching of other believers. Preachers and teachers through sermons, presentations, and writing have expounded on the Bible. The Bible teaches that these sources are part of God's gift to the church and a provision from Him. This valuable information requires thinking. We need to determine its relevance to application in our life. We need to see how it addresses the mystery of who I am or how things work.

This thinking process leads us toward a settled belief. Here is an interesting phenomenon. I have often experienced, and I suspect that most people have, that sometimes when rereading a passage of scripture or an author who is a believer, suddenly I gain a new or additional insight that further refines a belief. Often this comes from a connection being made with other information in my knowledge bank. I believe that is an example of the progressive nature of movement in the mystery of godliness toward becoming more godly and is the work of the indwelling Holy Spirit. Literally, this is God speaking to us.

Thinking

Let's back up and be a little more general about the thinking that surrounds beliefs. Remember there are two categories: **truth** and **not-truth**. There are specific truths that are taught in the Bible and additional truths that are connected to creation and this current age. A truth for this current age is the sun rises in the east and sets in the west. Now, I know this has to do with the rotation of the earth and not the movement of the sun.

However, for the point of this illustration, we operate daily on the truth of sunrise and sunset. We operate on the reliability of the truth of gravity. We have many mathematical equations that we depend upon in our life.

There are many complex operations within my computer that I depend upon as I am typing. I don't understand most of them, but we even say our computer has an operating system. Since there is a one-to-one correspondence between which key I strike and the letter that appears on the screen, I am able to produce words. This is how computers work in this world even though most of it is a mystery to most of us.

We can proceed with our daily lives depending on the detailed things we believe and the thinking that supports them. In summary, we think to arrive at a belief, we think to analyze a belief and we think to revise a belief. We rely on our knowledge base as a source for that thinking and use the marvelous brains that the Lord has given us.

What thinking that is involved in the drive part of the belief drives practice principle? A good reminder is to recall that much of this thinking is something of which we are not particularly aware. Perhaps this is a good place to introduce a principle from Dallas Willard that is very similar to the principle of belief drives practice. He has a principle called VIM. The "V" is for vision, the "I" is for intention and the "M" is for means. Vision kind of parallels belief, intention parallels drive, and means parallels practice.

We cannot visualize without thinking, and usually the thinking is very focused. Also, usually the focus is thinking about what or how something ought to be. We are visualizing a positive situation or outcome. This visualization about the belief sets the stage for the commitment to move into drive or intention. It all starts in our head.

The thinking surrounding drive does involve the will and intention because the drive involves the movement. If you drive a vehicle, it is understood that the vehicle moves, or if you drive a horse we understand that the horse moves. Drive turns the belief into practice. In the drive part of the principle, we are thinking about how we are going to perform the practice. We may be thinking about when we are going to perform the practice. We may be thinking about what the practice will look like.

Just like the thinking around belief, we will rely on our knowledge bank as a resource for thinking about the drive part of the principle. It is good to point out that the knowledge bank contains content around previous experiences. In summary, the thinking about drive is centered on the choice of moving to practice, the action that will be required to perform the practice and the possible costs or risks related to the practice.

Lastly, let's look into the thinking involved in the practice part of our principle—belief drives practice. Obviously, there is thinking involved in performing the practice whether the practice is thought, word, or deed. We think about what will be required to perform the practice. Are there steps and sequences to follow? Are there materials or resources required? Is there a timetable involved? Are there other people to be considered? Are there costs to be considered? Once again, the knowledge and the experience bank will play its role.

Let's walk through a recent simple experience of mine as an illustration. Recently, on a Friday afternoon, my Amish neighbor called seeking a ride to the tractor supply company. He had a broken part on his baler, and he wanted to be able to bale hay that night. He asked if I were available, and since I was relaxing and watching a recorded football game, I was available. Since my belief is God wants me to love my neighbor, and since I want to obey the Lord, I was driven to say yes.

I had to think about whether I was available and briefly if I had the means. The answer was yes to both thoughts. I had to remember that God wanted me to love my neighbor, and as a matter of fact, I commented to my wife that the Lord had provided me an opportunity to love my neighbor.

I had to think about which vehicle to take to town. I decided to take the pickup rather than the car because I wasn't certain about the size of the part he was picking up. I had to think about the process of getting the pickup out of the garage. I had to think about the route to take to town after I picked my neighbor up at his home. I had to think about all the operations of driving the pickup and of course the same thinking pattern happened in reverse for the trip home, including parking the pickup back in the garage.

In this illustration I have demonstrated some of the thinking involved in this simple transaction involved in the principle of belief drives practice. I could have gone into much more detail, but I think this suffices to illustrate the thinking process. You probably observed that it is not always really clear which thinking goes with each step in the principle. I don't think this matters because clearly there is thinking involved throughout the process.

Just think about how automatically most of this happens. Once again, the marvelous brain that our Creator has given us has equipped us to function in the quest of mystery of godliness. Much of the process is not particularly glamorous or sensational; rather it looks like resting and abiding.

New Thinking

Let's look at and explore a verse that provides an example of how the new mind of the transformed believer works.

> *Let him that stole steal no more: but rather let him labour, working with his hands the thing which is good, that he may have to give to him that is in need* (Romans 4:28).

Let's begin with the question: When is a thief not a thief? A quick answer might be: When he is not stealing. However, he may not be stealing because he currently lacks an opportunity to steal or perhaps is relaxing and enjoying whatever he has recently stolen. We can be a little absurd and say that the thief is on a vacation.

Now let's talk about what a thief is actually doing when he steals. Simply put, the thief is taking someone else's stuff without their permission. In the case of a robbery, the thief is forcefully taking the other person's possession while a sneak thief is taking a person's possession and avoiding detection in the act of stealing.

How did the victim of the thief acquire the possessions that have been stolen? The possessions may have been received by the victim as a gift or an inheritance but most often the possessions were purchased with earnings the victim received by working somewhere.

Let's move to the scripture and focus on the word "rather." The word rather is a transition word to move our thinking from stealing to something else. The suggestion is for the thief to move from stealing what he wants to laboring to earn what he wants. This is a good change of direction.

Instead of working at stealing, the person who was a thief switches to laboring to earn. Instead of taking the fruit of another person's labor, now the ex-thief is laboring to earn what he wants. Notice the scripture does not stop with change of direction. The scripture goes on to say that the ex-thief will take the fruit of their earnings and use it to give to those in need.

Back to our question: When is a thief not a thief? The answer: A thief is no longer a thief when instead of being a *taker* he becomes a *giver*. The ex-thief has changed his belief system. He has replaced the **not-truth** belief that it's okay to steal another person's property with a **truth** belief that is good to give to the needs of another person.

> *I have shewed you all things, how that so laboring ye ought to support the weak, and to remember the words of the Lord Jesus, how he said, It is more blessed to give than to receive* (Acts 20:35).

There we have it! We now know when a thief is no longer a thief. We also have a great example about how a change in belief results in a change in practice. The old belief that stealing was okay resulted in the practice of stealing another's possessions. The new belief in laboring to earn so that one can give resulted in the practice of giving to the needs of others.

Transforming is changing. We can see that the "trans" part of the word relates to moving. Believers who are transforming are moving from less godly to more godly. It is a process and we can see it is a work of God facilitated by intentional activity in beliefs by the believer. Can you understand better what you are experiencing?

Chapter 12

Deeper Problems

These things I have spoken unto you, that in me ye might have peace. In the world ye shall have tribulation: but be of good cheer; I have overcome the world (John 16:33).

Now let's take a backward look at our principle of belief drives practice. We can observe a practice, which is visible, and be assured that there is a belief, which is invisible, that is driving the practice. Let's not forget that sometimes the word "behavior" makes for a clearer understanding than "practice."

Remember back when I mentioned how my mentor, Jim Wright, had stated that you can judge a person's practice (behavior) but not their hearts because only God knows their hearts. Scripture says,

Wherefore by their fruits ye shall know them (Matthew 7:20).

For man looketh on the outward appearance, but the Lord looketh on the heart (1 Sam. 16:7).

I think this is why in Proverbs there are many verses that identify fools and their foolish behaviors and attitudes, and yet we are instructed to call no man a fool. This is an important caution as we observe a person's practice.

Let's get personal. Our goal in exploring the mystery of godliness is to discover how we personally can be transformed into godly behavior. Our focus needs to be on reflecting on our own practice, particularly the practices that we do not think are really very godly. We may be under conviction from the Holy Spirit about these practices that are concerning us.

When we apply our principle of belief drives practice, we must assume there is some belief we hold that is driving that practice. Our first assumption is we are holding a belief that is not the truth. Said another way, we are not holding a belief that is the truth. The solution is clear, discard the belief that is not the truth and replace it with a belief that is the truth. This sounds so easy.

Moving ahead with the belief exchange theory, which is sometimes not so easy. First of all, we can't insert the belief that is the truth if we don't know what the truth is. This is a case of personal ignorance. Ignorance sounds negative, but the good news is it can be removed with knowledge acquired through learning.

A number of times in the scriptures the Apostle Paul stated, *"I would not have you ignorant brethren."* He then proceeds to teach them some relevant truth. Part of what makes this lack of knowledge a difficult problem is we don't know what we don't know.

I think that if we come to a place where we desire to change a practice but can't figure out where our belief is incorrect, we ask the Lord first, and in some cases, we may want to ask someone in whom we have confidence. Sometimes someone will give you the correction unsolicited. This is not always comfortable.

The Hard Stuff

In my training and practice as a counselor in talk therapy, a foundational concept was: through talk therapy a counselor was to help

Deeper Problems

a client discover their thinking behind their presenting problem. There is an assumed cause and effect in place. It is assumed that there is a cause behind the undesired effect (the presenting problem).

This is how it would work: a client comes to a counselor with what they perceive as the presenting problem. Said another way, the client is having significant problems with either their perception of who they are or struggles with how their world is not working for them.

We use the concept "presenting problem" because it may be discovered that the presenting problem is not the root problem. Often this is the case. Also, obviously we use the term presenting problem because that is what the client sees as the problem. Through a series of probing questions, the counselor will seek to guide the client into thinking about their beliefs and behaviors that are linked to the presenting problem.

If these beliefs and behaviors are successfully identified, the counselor continues to guide the client into discovering how these beliefs are contributing to the presenting problem and ultimately to change those beliefs and behaviors into ones that will alleviate the presenting problem. This sounds very straightforward and even a little mechanical. It should be easy to see that this therapy process is based on the principle: belief drives practice.

For most of us the many times in our lives when we experience problems with our practices, we are able to ask our own probing questions, discover our error in belief and thinking, change to a different belief or way of thinking, and produce a practice that is acceptable.

For a simple example: A person is attempting a task and they have a plan (belief) that drives the implementation of the plan but the product (practice) turns out to not be what was desired. The usual response is to go back to the drawing board and come up with plan "B." They go through the process of implementing the new plan and if the product is satisfactory, problem solved. However, there are those problems that defy our ability to find the solution of a better way of thinking. For these we need help.

There are practices that are seriously disruptive and troubling for a person in the quest for discovering who they are and may manifest as depression, addiction, anger, loss of sleep, or in other ways. When a person cannot figure "it" out, help is needed.

For our purposes of discussion, we are assuming that both the client and the counselor are believers. In this setting both should be committed to the value of the word of God as a resource and believe that God the Holy Spirit is dwelling in both client and counselor and is actively involved in resolving the problem(s).

Resolution is part of the path to godly behavior in the mystery of godliness. It may not be easy to discover the wrong belief that needs to be replaced with the right belief. The client may not only be confused but also in denial about what they actually believe.

Sometimes the wrong belief is deeply seated in the client because the origin may have come from a traumatic event or been deeply imprinted by a person of authority. If the person of authority was also abusive, you have both deep imprinting and trauma. Usually there are strong emotions linked with the beliefs, particularly the emotion of fear. Similar dynamics are in play if the presenting problem is connected to answering the question, how does the world work?

Deeper Problems

It is important to insert that the model of counselor and client is not the only application for this discussion because the relationship between counselor and client may not be formal, but the counselor could be a friend or teacher and the client could be a friend or a student.

Sometimes the counselor can be an author of a book that is relevant to the issue. We even have a name for this called bibliotherapy. We can even think of our reading of the Bible as a practice of bibliotherapy. As the truth impacts and changes our beliefs, we gain the benefits of more godly practices.

Dr. Larry Crabb addresses his therapeutic process as the wrong beliefs being a wrong set of tapes playing in a person's mind. The person keeps hearing these tapes playing, which of course would drive the undesired practices. The solution is to replace the wrong tapes with the right tapes so that the person hears the truth playing in their mind.

Another model that is sometimes used is the concept of "reframing." In visualizing this concept think about a picture frame. The frame encloses a scene. The goal of reframing is to get a different view of the scene by changing what is enclosed. For discovering the right and true way of thinking and believing sometimes this model is helpful.

In summary, the principle of belief drives practice has a fundamental application for addressing seriously disturbing problems in practice. This is confirming the validity of the principle of belief drives practice. This discussion also demonstrates that undesirable practice can be the catalyst to exploring current beliefs and changing those beliefs to align with the truth. It also contributes to our understanding of how the renewing of the minds of believers is transforming them into the image of Christ toward more godly behavior.

We have used the concept of clues to help in solving the mystery, but in this chapter, we have look at clues to discover **not-truth** thinking that is disruptive. Are you getting the sense that there are many aspects to understanding the transforming journey and can you still see that it is a process?

Chapter 13

Finding Freedom

For several years, my wife and I had cattle. We would purchase calves in the spring, pasture them all summer, and sell them in fall. After purchasing them we would keep them in the corral for a few days to be sure they were healthy and didn't need any doctoring. One year after turning the calves out to pasture, we held a couple of calves back in the corral for a while.

When we turned the last two out with the rest of the herd, it produced an amazing sight to see. These two calves ran around the pasture, tails in the air, bucking and jumping as they dashed around among the other members of the herd. It was hilarious to watch. It was as if they were saying, "Free at last, free at last!"

Would You Be Free from Your Burden of Sin?
There's pow'r in the blood, pow'r in the blood;
Would you o'er evil a victory win?
There's pow'r in the blood.
Would you be free from your passion and pride?
There's pow'r in the blood, pow'r in the blood:
Come for a cleansing to Calvary's tide?
There's pow'r in the blood.
Would you be whiter, much whiter than snow?
There's pow'r in the blood, pow'r in the blood:
Sin stains are lost in the life giving flow;

There's pow'r in the blood.
Would you do service for Jesus your King?
There's pow'r in the blood, pow'r in the blood:
Would you like daily His praises to sing?
There's pow'r in the blood.

Let's ponder truth for a while and start by looking at the following verse from John.

> *Then said Jesus to those Jews which believed on him, If ye continue in my word, then ye are my disciples; And ye shall know the truth, and the truth shall make you free* (John 8: 31-32).

There is a relationship between truth and freedom. I think we can safely conclude that freedom is a good and desirable thing. Let's think of freedom as being free *from* something and also as being free *to* something.

The above hymn speaks of the freedom from judgment for sin and being free from passion and pride, as well as freedom to sing His praises. The burden of sin seems to speak of the weight of judgment from sin and the sacrifice of Jesus through His blood frees us from His righteous judgment because He paid the penalty for our sin. This is clear from the scriptures.

Guilt and Shame

However, another burden of sin is the sense of guilt we carry. With awareness of having sinned comes a sense of guilt. It is a package deal; they come together. A sinner feels guilty because the sinner is guilty. Often, if not usually, guilt carries with it the burden of shame. Shame can be a heavy burden! Look at this description from John Eldredge's book, *Captivating:*

Shame enters in and makes its crippling home deep within our hearts. Shame is what makes us look away, so we avoid eye contact with strangers and friends. Shame is that feeling that haunts us, the sense that if someone really knew us, they would shake their heads in disgust and run away. Shame makes us feel, no, *believe*, that we do not measure up—not to the world's standards, the church's standard, or our own (p. 73).

We know from I John 1:9 that confession of the sin to the Lord is followed by His forgiveness and cleansing. *"If we confess our sins, he is faithful and just to forgive us our sins, and to cleanse us from all unrighteousness."* The sense of guilt will be removed if we believe what the verse says that we are forgiven and cleansed. Unfortunately, sometimes the sense of guilt does not seem to go away even after we have confessed our sin. Why is that?

Let's look at our principle: belief drives practice. If a person is feeling guilty, that is practice and evidence that there is a problem with the belief. In some way the error in belief is that the Lord has not responded to confession with forgiveness and cleansing. Clearly this person is believing the **not-truth**—that the Lord did not forgive and cleanse. The solution is to change the belief to the truth from scripture that the Lord has forgiven and cleansed. Why might it be so hard to not continue to feel guilty?

Although there could be several reasons, one main reason may be that the sense of guilt is focused on how the person sees the sin. The sin may seem particularly bad and just plain awful. The sin may have resulted in others being hurt. The sin may have been embarrassing and very shaming. The sin may have been very public. The sin may have been a crime. The person may get all caught up in a need to forgive themselves or to be forgiven by others. The bottom line is that the sin and guilt issues are between the individual and their Lord.

The transaction remains: believe the Lord will forgive following confessed sin and cleansing of the sinner, and fellowship and relationship is restored between the individual and the Lord. Hence, praise the Lord, there is freedom from the burden of sin. There still may be some natural consequences from the sin that will occur, but this does not preclude the restoration of relationship with the Lord through confession.

False Guilt

While we are on the subject of the bondage of guilt, let's look at another kind of guilt that can capture a person. This is false guilt. Often in talk therapy the counselor needs to help the counselee recognize how they are imprisoned with false guilt. What is false guilt? Simply put: false guilt is feeling guilty for something for which you are not guilty.

Here is an example: Sometimes when a couple divorces, their child will assume that somehow, they caused the divorce. It doesn't matter that neither the father nor the mother ever blamed the child; the child may still feel guilty. This is somewhat understandable because often children are very concrete and see themselves as the cause of everything about them. This sense that they are the cause of everything may be reinforced in their minds by the frequent and normal correction they receive from their parents.

This belief of a false guilt can carry on into adulthood. This belief in a **not-truth** causes problems because the guilt-ridden child will proceed to punish themselves. This belief in the **not-truth** also creates a problem for the confession-forgiveness-cleansing solution. How can a person be forgiven for a sin that they did not commit?

Hence, there is no relief for the guilt, and self-imposed punishment follows. To make matters even worse since the self-imposed punishment is based on false guilt, the punishment can never be sufficient because the false guilt remains. Therefore, punishment must go on and on. What bondage!

Let's stop for some analysis. There is the basic understanding that the guilty should be punished. That is why forgiveness from the Lord is so prized because it provides an escape from punishment. In the courts, the sentence from the judge follows the verdict of guilty. After the sentence is served, we say justice has been served, the criminal is free to go and return to society.

While serving as an elementary school principal, I had the opportunity and responsibility to discipline students. Frequently, the punishment for the student guilty of some infraction in the classroom, in the hall, or on the playground was to "serve time" sitting in my office. At the conclusion of the "time served," the student would be returned to the classroom. The student, having served his sentence, was restored to good standing, and there was no need for the student to feel guilty. All was well. Justice was served. You could say there had been a cleansing. The goal has been that the discipline will be an instructional experience.

> *Now no chastening for the present seemeth to be joyous, but grievous: nevertheless afterward it yieldeth the peaceable fruit of righteousness unto them which are exercised by it* (Hebrews 12:11).

Another source of false guilt is created by blaming. Sometimes one person blames another person for something that the person did not do. If the person being blamed believes the accuser, the false guilt pattern occurs. Essentially, the false guilt becomes a burden with the negative effects described above. The false guilt burden can become a burden that a person can carry for many years and result in serious disruptive suffering. These effects can have a significant impact on relationships with others. Sometimes the blaming takes the form of what I call, "emotional loading." When this happens, one person seeks to make another person responsible for their emotions.

For example: a parent blames a child for making them mad or sad. The child may be guilty of the misbehavior that does affect the parent's emotions, but blaming has the effect of assigning responsibility for the parent's emotions to the child. Two things happen. The child is loaded with a burden of false guilt. In a perverse way, the child has been given the assignment of caring for the parent rather than the parent caring for the child as it should be.

The misbehavior that needed to be addressed properly gets lost. The child goes away feeling guilty about the wrong thing. The parent should take responsibility for their own emotions, and the child should take responsibility for their own misbehavior. This has been a simplistic example and often it is more complex than this, but the problem of false guilt caused by blaming is very common. The belief in the **not-truth** drives the practice of a burden of false guilt.

How does this apply to our journey to godliness? Godliness is built on believing the truth with godly practice to follow. Any **not-truths** will interfere with our journey. Once again, the mystery of godliness comes into play because the Holy Spirit through the application of the truth will guide us into freedom. The truth will make us free!

Freedom From

Now, let's explore the concept of freedom by looking at freedom "from." If a person is not free, they are confined, a captive, a prisoner, trapped, restricted, or regulated. An outside force is somehow restricting freedom. Just imagine how Peter felt.

Finding Freedom

And when Herod would have brought him forth, the same night Peter was sleeping between two soldiers, bound with two chains: and the keepers before the door kept the prison. And, behold, the angel of the Lord came upon him, and a light shined in the prison: and he smote Peter on the side, and raised him up, saying, Arise up quickly. And his chains fell off from his hands (Acts 12: 6-7).

The children of Israel were slaves in Egypt. They wanted to be free to worship God. Although not exactly slaves, the serfs of the Middle Ages did not have freedom. Until the Emancipation Proclamation in the United States, slavery existed and was legal. History is filled with horrifying stories about the treatment of prisoners of war.

Today oppressive and controlling countries impose restrictions on their citizens. All of these people lacked freedom from living their lives as they please. Freedom is very important to Americans. Look at our War of Independence from England. Look at this language from the Declaration of Independence:

> We hold these truths to be self-evident, that all men are created equal, that they are endowed by their Creator with certain unalienable Rights, that among these are Life, Liberty and the pursuit of Happiness.—That to secure these rights, Governments are instituted among Men, deriving their just powers from the consent of the governed, —That whenever any Form of Government becomes destructive of these ends, it is the Right of the People to alter or to abolish it, and to institute new Government, laying its foundation on such principles and organizing its powers in such form, as to them shall seem most likely to affect their Safety and Happiness.

The declaration is based on self-evident truths that originate with our Creator. Our forefathers would go on to codify many freedoms into the Constitution, and many of the amendments go on to declare specific freedoms.

On a lighter side we look further at freedoms, both freedoms from and freedoms to. Students are released from the confinement of the classroom to the freedom of recess. Throughout my career I have attended many professional conferences, which are usually fairly tightly scheduled, but almost always "free time" from the sessions is scheduled where attendees are free to do what they want rather than attend sessions.

I retired from the eight-to-five employments after many years. Now I am free from having to meet the schedule of being to work at a specific time and free to get up and do what I want when I want. No need to set the alarm clock. It was an adjustment—but what a sense of freedom!

People who are self-employed are free from the demands of answering to an employer and free to operate their business as they wish. This is not to ignore that there are responsibilities and requirements in operating a successful business that seem to restrict the freedom of the self-employed. Basketball players are awarded a free throw when they have been fouled by an opponent. In baseball, a runner gets a free base when the pitcher balks.

There is a legal process in which minor children can receive emancipation from their parents. The child is free from the authority and responsibility of their parents and free to function as adults. In each of these examples there is a truth that generates the freedom.

There are rules that can withhold freedom and rules that provide exceptions that give freedom. There is truth in both the rules and the exceptions. Free time at recess or at a conference occurs because of the truth of the rules and exceptions. The truth about the reality of retirement gives the freedom to not have to report to work. The truth of being self-employed provides the freedom from answering to an employer. The ball players get something free because of the truth of the rules of the game. The emancipation papers are the truth that frees a child from their parents.

Here are some more examples: Our Amish neighbors have some goats, and most of the goats have horns. Often the goats will stick their heads through the woven wire fence to graze, and then when they try to remove their heads, their horns hang up on the wire fence. The goats let the whole neighborhood know about their dilemma with a pathetic bleating.

Both my wife and I have rescued them many times, and even more times we have called the neighbors to let them know that a goat was caught. Upon releasing the goat, the goat has its freedom, at least until the next time.

We acquired some barn cats to help with rodent control and in the interest of cat population control, we wanted to get the cats neutered. Problem: the cats were not tame enough for us to catch, and they loved their freedom. We acquired some live traps from some friends; and on the second attempt, we were able to trap the cats. Upon returning from the vets, the cats were released from the traps and really enjoyed their freedom.

We have corrals for our sheep and our horses. The corrals have gates. The gates act as the truth because when opened, the animals are free to go to pasture; and when closed, the animals are not free to leave the corral. There are places in the western United States that are called open range. Livestock are free to wander as they wish. Often warning signs are placed along roads that pass through open range areas. It seems natural for us to love our freedom.

Perhaps you will remember Willie Nelson's famous song, written years ago by Gene Autry, entitled "Don't Fence Me In." In it was a cowboy's plea that he be able to ride through the country without any restrictions, free of fences.

Fear

We love to hear proclamations of freedom. You are debt free! You are cancer free! You are pain free! You are addiction free. This truth is such good news because debt, cancer, pain and addiction had been holding a person captive.

Fear is another captor that holds us until we are freed by the truth. Fear of anything can capture us. Fear of loss of health, possessions, money, loved ones, our life or safety can plague us. What is the answer? Any of these losses that we fear can happen.

> *There is no fear in love; but perfect love casteth out fear: because fear has torment. He that feareth is not made perfect in love* (I John 4:18).

The truth of the power of love is our antidote to fear. When we apply our principle, belief drives practice, we see that our practice is fear, and we must conclude that we are lacking in believing in perfect love. Only belief in God's love is the perfect love that is needed. Do we fear dying?

> *...that through death he might destroy him that had the power of death, that is, the devil; And deliver them who through fear of death were all their lifetime subject to bondage* (Hebrews 2:14-15).

There you have it! We can experience freedom from the bondage of the fear of death because the Lord Jesus experienced death for us. It seems that many fears are based on failure to really believe in the goodness of God toward us. Maybe because my wife and I have sheep, we often are able to make reference and connections with sheep and the shepherd, particularly in light of the fact the Lord Jesus is our shepherd, and we are his sheep.

My wife made the observation that, "We tend to act as if we didn't have a shepherd." I think this is profound. Follow me with this! The shepherd of John 10 cares for his sheep. He provides their food and protects them from danger. He even goes after them if they get lost. We can be free from fear of lack or need or danger by relying on the truth that the Lord is in control and has full capacity to respond on our behalf to each fear.

I am the good shepherd: the good shepherd giveth his life for the sheep (John 10:11).

I am the good shepherd, and know my sheep, and am known of mine. As the Father knoweth me, even so know I the Father: and I lay down my life for the sheep. And other sheep I have, which are not of this fold: them also I must bring, and they shall hear my voice; and there shall be one fold, and one shepherd (John 10:14-16).

Jesus Christ proclaimed His ministry by quoting Isaiah 61:1-3:

The Spirit of the Lord God is upon me; because the Lord hath appointed me to preach good tidings unto the meek; he hath sent me to bind up the brokenhearted, to proclaim liberty to the captives, and opening of the prison to them that are bound; To proclaim the acceptable year of the Lord, and the day of vengeance of our God; to comfort all who mourn; to appoint unto them that mourn in Zion, to give unto them beauty for ashes, the oil of joy for mourning, the garment of praise for the spirit of heaviness; that they might be called the trees of righteousness, the planting of the Lord, that he might be glorified.

Now that mission covers all our fears. The Lord is saying, "I've got this!" Since this is the truth, all we have to do is believe it. If we believe it, we will be able to practice a faithful rest and freedom from fear with confidence in our Lord.

Often slaves who have no freedom are pictured in chains. I like the vision of chains falling off! Have you had the experience of the chains falling off?

Chapter 14

Seeking Truth

> The test of God's truth is that it fits you exactly, if it does not, question whether it is His truth (Oswald Chambers, *My Utmost for His Highest*).

We are going to explore the concept of the truth further. Everyone has an innate desire to seek the truth. We have a thirst for truth. The Lord has given us inquiring minds with a desire to learn. We are curious. This is a good thing!

Each one has a deep-seated belief that there is truth. The desire to seek the truth drives a person to the practice of discovering the truth. Then if the discovered truth has relevance, the belief in this truth will drive the practice as we have discussed before. The deep desire to discover and know the truth will be our focus. Where does this come from? Brace yourself because before we seek to answer that question, I am going to wear the concept of truth seeking to death.

Think about how scientists, detectives, and researchers diligently pursue discovering the truth in their area of interest. Let's look at scientists first. The scientist starts with a hypothesis about what they are trying to discover or a problem they are wanting to solve. The hypothesis is an educated guess, and the scientist will look for evidence to support the hypothesis. The whole process is based on the assumption that there is truth to be found.

My wife and I enjoy watching many of the documentaries on the television shows like *Nature* and *Nova*. Apart from the distraction of ridiculous proclamations about evolution or attributing divine qualities to nature, the content can be very interesting. Generally, the photography is fantastic.

Recently we watched an episode on *Nova* about research on the intelligence of birds. The story outlined recent discoveries and the changes in researchers' thinking about birds being more intelligent than previously thought and that the birds' behavior was not just instinct. The researchers were very intensely committed to their work. Some seemed almost obsessed and had been working with birds for many years. The facilities where they worked were very impressive. Clearly, the assumption was that there was a truth about birds' intelligence and through diligent research that truth could be found.

Although very interesting information, I wondered, Why is it important to discover bird intelligence? What difference will it make? How will this discovery be useful? There may be answers to these questions, but they were not addressed in the program. Then some further questions came to my mind that probably come from my experience as a school administrator. Who is paying for all of this? How is it funded? My assumption was there is a truth that will answer my questions.

Let's look at detectives. My wife and I like to watch detective mystery shows on television. We speculate on why this is, and we have talked about why we like them. One of our conclusions is we like the fact that the bad guys get caught. That doesn't always happen in real life. Also, the stories are presented in such a way that the viewer is involved in following the clues to help solve the case. The quest in solving the mystery is based on the assumption that there is undiscovered truth that awaits discovery, and the skill and wits of the detective will be able to put it all together and reach the true solution. Hence, the truth will come out!

The really intriguing stories seem to suggest a number of suspects as the villain to keep the audience and the detectives guessing. The final climax of the story is the ability of the brilliant detective to discover what others may have missed and properly identify the culprit. Success—the truth has been discovered.

We have been discussing fiction. In real life you also see ardent searching for the truth by the authorities when a crime has been committed. Often sketches, pictures, or surveillance pictures are released asking for the public's help for leads on the suspects. This is a search for the truth. In 2017 a shooter opened fire on an audience at a concert in Las Vegas. The shooter, who had many weapons and much ammunition, fired from a vantage point in a high-rise hotel that overlooked the concert. Many people were killed and many more were wounded.

As is often the case in these types of incidents, the shooter killed himself. There has been ongoing investigation into the killer's motives. In spite of many interviews and examination of the killer's electronic devices, his motives are still unknown. The FBI says it will take a year before they can determine his motive.

Why this obsession with knowing his motives? What difference will it make? The killer is dead and that knowledge will not bring any of his victims back to life. There is a drive to discover the truth. I can understand a need to know if there were accomplices or if there was some further danger, but once it was determined that there were no accomplices or further danger, why keep pressing? I believe it is our innate desire to discover truth.

Closely related to crime investigation and the search for the truth is the area of unsolved crimes. Often highlighted in news stories about unsolved crimes and cold cases is the notion that the grieving relatives and friends of the victim will somehow experience some sense of relief if the crime is solved. Not knowing the truth about what happened and the identity of the person who was responsible for the crime increase their pain. Very similar anguish is experienced by people who have relatives or friends who have disappeared. There is a longing for the truth about the lost person.

Researchers are in a search for the truth. Honest researchers are very committed to the accuracy of their work. Through the years I have taught an educational research course at three different universities. There are very specific guidelines and protocols in conducting and reporting research findings. There are formulas and emphases concerning validity and reliability. Research can be peer reviewed and should be able to duplicate yielding the same results. All of this is evidence of commitment to discovering truth.

Why do you think quiz shows are so popular? My wife and I like to watch Jeopardy. The challenge of guessing the correct answer is very stimulating. The correct answer is the truth. We are able to guess some the answers, but the contestants usually beat us to the correct answers that we actually know. The whole premise of the show is identifying the truthful answer to questions, and actually on Jeopardy they do it backwards because the answer given by the contestants is in the form of a question to the presented clue. The point is that the thirst to know the truth is being gratified in a nonthreatening way.

Losses

The search for lost items is an attempt to find the truth of where the item is located. For years I have entertained and sometimes irritated people who are looking for a lost item with my clever statement (at least in my own mind it is clever). I say, "I know where you will find it." Usually, the person with the lost item excitedly responds with the question, "Where?" My clever response is: "In the last place you look." A little levity can ease the tension. Sure, enough I am proved to be right and usually a chuckle follows.

My point is that searching for lost items is part of a search for truth. At times I have mislaid or lost a tool or an item, and I find myself troubled even though I may actually have another tool that could work or it is not essential to find the lost tool because it can be easily replaced. Why is that? Because I am driven to know the truth about where the item is located. Again, that innate drive to know the truth.

Let's explore a more serious example of seeking the truth about losses. My sister-in-law died in an accident when she was in her fifties. The first search for truth was related to how the accident happened. What were the details? The next search for truth centered around why God would allow this to happen.

This second question can lead into an area of acceptance of the Lord's sovereign will and accepting that, in spite of the pain of the loss, the Lord is good and His will is perfect. There is a danger that in a desperate search for the truth, a person may fall into Satan's trap and blame God. That is not good. The drive to know the truth continues even in the face of the fact that this knowledge would not make a difference in the end result.

These searches can be fueled by the pain of mourning and

lamenting. We believe that somehow if the truth can be discovered about some details surrounding the loss, we will find relief. Here is a verse that I have found comforting in these trying times.

Fear not, little flock; for it is your Father's good pleasure to give you the kingdom (Luke 12: 32).

Solutions

One more example of the search for the truth can be found in the area of problem solving. Everyone has experience in problem solving. Sometimes the problems are rather simple and mundane, and thankfully that is mostly the case. Other times the problems can be very complex and hard to solve. The assumption is always that there is truth to be found leading to the solution of the problem.

For the complex problems, we may have to seek the assistance of a specialist or expert. One day our refrigerator was not functioning properly. I had to locate an appliance repairman who came to our house and found the truth of the problem. He fixed it by replacing a broken component in the computer controls of the refrigerator. All it took to solve the problem was $340 and Ivan's expertise. Oh well, it was less expensive than a new refrigerator. Problem solving is a skill that can be taught. Here is an example of a problem-solving plan or technique in steps.

- Identify the problem.
- Explore information and create ideas.
- Select the best idea.
- Build and test the idea.
- Evaluate the results.
- If the results are not acceptable, go through the steps again.

Seeking Truth

The point is that the search for truth is integrated into our lives. The search for the truth is usually based on questions to be answered. Think over the many examples we have just discussed, and almost always there was a search for an answer to a question. When we are searching for the truth in any context, there is an inward restlessness that only the truth can settle.

Another way to think about the search for truth is it is like an itch that can only be relieved by discovering the truth. Now how does this barrage of discussion about truth relate to our topic, the mystery of godliness?

Before moving on in this exploration of truth, let's look at the nature of the questions that are seeking truth. I think that is some way each seeking question is linked to our desire to answer these questions that we first identified in our discussion about our self-system: Who am I? How do I work? How does the world work? And for the believers: How does the Kingdom of God work?

Stop and think about our creation. We are created in the image of God and then came the fall of mankind. For the first time, man and God were separated. Adam and Eve tried to hide from God, but the Lord came searching for them. Adam and Eve were hiding because they knew that they had sinned and disobeyed God.

There is innately deep inside every man a desire to know God, and it is not possible to know God except in the realm of the truth. God is truth. Although the Lord takes the initiative to seek us and has revealed Himself to us in both His creation and His scriptures, there is still is a desire to discover the truth that can only be found in God. Although Satan has sought to contradict and confuse this search for truth with lies and false religions, the desire still remains.

There is a yearning for restoration deep inside every person. I believe it is placed there by God, and it is part of being an image bearer. Sin, Satan, and false religions can definitely interfere and numb, misplace, or distract this yearning; but it exists. Scripture warns that it is also possible to quench the Spirit. *"Quench not the Spirit"* (2 Thessalonians 5: 19).

At the same time, we, like Adam and Eve, will also be inclined to hide from God. We know we are sinners and feel guilty and have a fear of God's judgment. There is an internal conflict between wanting to know the truth as found in God and to avoid His righteous judgment. Praise be to God there is the solution of coming to Him!

> *The Lord is not slack concerning his promise, as some men count slackness; but is longsuffering to us-ward, not willing that any should perish, but that all should come to repentance* (2 Peter 3:9).

This deep desire to know the truth is a precious gift from God. This inward drive for truth sets us up to be receptive to His seeking us. This is part of the mystery of godliness. We are talking about the meeting of our deep desire for truth that leads to knowing God and God's seeking us for restoration and relationship. What does it feel like? What does it look like? Once again, we are entering the realm of *"other"* and *"beyond."*

C. S. Lewis in his *Tales of Narnia* has the Lord symbolized as the lion, Aslan. In the stories the scene is set for the appearance of Aslan by the characters sensing that Aslan is moving in the land. In the mystery of godliness, when the Holy Spirit is providing guidance to the believer, it is something like that. The believer may not be able to clearly explain that the Spirit of God is guiding, but the believer knows. This is the precious experience of believers who see the mystery of godliness happening in their lives.

Seeking Truth

Howbeit when he, the Spirit of truth, is come, he will guide you into all truth: for he shall not speak of himself; but whatsoever he shall hear, that shall he speak: and he will shew you things to come (John 16:13).

I believe that everything I am writing is true. I believe that what I am writing is a compilation of the truth I have been seeking for many years, and it is revelation from God to me during those years. When I was thinking about this idea, I thought about using the word "conclusion" instead of compilation to describe my journey about what I have been seeking and learning through the years.

But it is not the conclusion because I am still seeking more understanding of the truth, and I am confident that the Spirit of God will continue to reveal more truth. It is a good thing that there is more to learn. It would be very presumptuous to think otherwise.

It is also delightful to look forward to continuing to learn truth. It is interesting as I reflect on the experience of writing my thoughts I become aware that the very act of gathering my thoughts on the mystery of godliness deepens my beliefs and grows my faith. Remember, the journey to godliness is a process that continues for all believers, but some day the understanding will be much more complete.

For now we see through a glass, darkly; but then face to face: now I know in part; but then shall I know even as also I am known (I Corinthians 13:12).

Chapter 15

God's Economy

"Be it unto you, even as you believe. In God's economy we believe first and then we see." —Joyce Meyer

The earth is the LORD'S, and the fulness thereof; the world, and they that dwell therein (Psalms 24:1).

We have discussed the concept of the renewing of the mind through the principle of belief drives practice that results in transformation. Now it is time to explore the application of truth from the scriptures into the believer belief system. We mentioned the concept of God's economy. By the word, economy, we simply mean the way things work in God's system.

First, we will look at God's economy in relation to theology. The scriptures teach basic concepts and basic relationships that are involved with God's relationship with mankind. A fundamental concept is God created everything including man. Man is a unique creation in that man was created in the image of God.

Let's pause and look more closely at what it means to be created in the image of God. J.I. Packer gives us some insight in his book, *Knowing God*:

This is what the Bible means when it tells us that God made man in His own image (Gen. 1:26f.) –namely, that God made man a free spiritual being, a responsible moral agent with powers to choose an action, able to commune with Him and respond to Him, and by nature good, truthful, holy, upright (cf. Eccles. 7:29): in a word godly.

The moral qualities which belonged to the divine image were lost in the Fall; God's image in man has been universally defaced, for all mankind has in one way or another lapsed into ungodliness. But the Bible tells us that now, in fulfilment of His plan of redemption, God is at work in believers to repair His ruined image by communicating these qualities to them afresh. This is what scripture means when it says that believers are being renewed in the image of Christ (2 Cor. 3:18) and of God (Col. 3:10) (pages 89-90).

Property Rights

Aligned with the fact of creation, is the principle that what is created is the property of the creator. This property right of the person who creates something is still in practice in cultures today (patents, trademarks, copyrights). The creator has no need to consult the creation about how the creation is created.

> *Nay but, O man, who art thou that repliest against God? Shall the thing formed say to Him that formed it, Why hast thou made me thus? Hath not the potter power over the clay, of the same lump to make one vessel unto honour, and another unto dishonor?* (Romans 9:20-21).

God is sovereign and He can do what He pleases with His creation. Clearly it is not ours to question. A clear application is the way we were made was God's prerogative. This includes the sex, the race, height, what we look like, the color of our eyes, the size of our ears, and the family of origin we were assigned. The truth is we are to accept how God made us and even when He made us. The choice about all of these details of "who we are" were His choices not ours.

In the Garden of Eden story, the scriptures explain the original sin and how sin came upon the human race—complete with the fall, death, and the curses. The doom of man could only be averted by a saving act by God. Early on we see that a blood sacrifice was required to provide redemption.

Throughout the Old Testament, there is a pattern of animal sacrifice for atonement that was clearly defined in the details of the Law of Moses. Scripture clearly explains that these blood sacrifices were only temporary and had to be repeated. These redemptive practices foreshadowed the advent of Christ's final and complete sacrifice of Himself that provided the complete salvation.

> *Neither by the blood of goats and calves, but by his own blood he entered in once into the holy place, having obtained eternal redemption for us* (Hebrews 9: 12).

In book after book of the Old Testament, we see the struggle with sin and disobedience of mankind. We see God's intervention and action both in rescue and in judgment. These lessons tell us much about both the nature of God and the nature of man the sinner. The application for today is for us to better understand who God is and how He interacts with mankind and to see how it applies in our personal lives and in the world around us today. This knowledge becomes part of our belief system.

In the New Testament, much explanation is given to contrasting the ways God related to the nation of the Jews with how He is relating to believers today. Scripture talks about the new covenant and the old covenant. The role of the law and how it relates to believers is discussed. We learn that no one is saved by the keeping of the law and that by the law is knowledge of sin. We also learn that the law is holy and true and that God has not recanted on the principles of holy behavior that the law requires.

However, we learn that with the advent of the Holy Spirit dwelling in believers a new and wonderful capacity has been given to enable believers to live godly lives.

We also learn about how things work in God's economy, which is a very big story of redemption and restoration. We learn there will be a new heaven and new earth. There will be a restoration of all things, a final judgment, and the removal of evil.

There is the big picture of what has happened, what is happening, and what will happen. With study of the scripture, we can identify where we fit into this big picture in the present time. All of this information provides the context that we need to formulate our belief system. God has not left us ignorant and unprepared to know Him and to live lives pleasing to Him.

Faith

The importance of faith as a factor in God's economy is a critical belief to establish in our belief system.

> *But without faith it is impossible to please Him* (Hebrews 11:6).

> *For whatsoever is not of faith is sin* (Romans 14:23).

> *Now faith is the substance of things hoped for, the evidence of things not seen* (Hebrews 11:1).

The eleventh chapter of Hebrews goes on to list a great honor roll of Bible characters who were examples of people demonstrating faith.

Another example of how God values faith is found in the fourteenth chapter of Romans. The issue being addressed is the differences in practices of different believers. Historically, these differences have led to serious divisions and conflicts between believers. Paul seeks to give us God's perspective on how much He values a person's faith as it relates to a commitment to please Him.

> *Him that is weak in the faith receive ye, but not to doubtful disputations. For one believeth that he may eat all things: another, who is weak, eateth herbs. Let not him that eateth despise him that eateth not; and let not him that eateth not judge him that eateth: for God has received him. How art thou that judgest another man's servant? To his own master he standeth or falleth. Yea, he shall be holden up: for God is able to make him stand. One man esteemeth one day above another: another esteemeth every day alike. Let every man be fully persuaded in his own mind. He that regardeth the day, regardeth it unto the Lord; and he that regardeth not the day, to the Lord he doth not regard it. He that eateth, eateth to the Lord, for he giveth God thanks; and he that eateth not, to the Lord he eateth not, and giveth God thanks (Romans 14:1-6).*

What we glean from this passage is how much God values the heart of the believer's desire to please Him. We can get caught up in the term of "who is weak" and miss the point of not judging another person's servant. When you stop and think about it, whether we are an eater or non-eater, we think the other one is the weaker. Assuming personal integrity, we would not choose to take what we see as the weaker position. We would be confident that our position is the proper decision and our practice is pleasing the Lord.

As I mentioned before, my home is surrounded by a community of Amish. Some of them are very good friends, and we have a great deal of interaction. We love them as neighbors and fellow believers. However, they have several unique customs, including the way they dress, the use of electricity, the use of horses, and non-ownership of vehicles and other customs.

I have no doubt in my mind that these practices are done based on a belief that they are pleasing the Lord. The differences between us and them are not a barrier to fellowship. The take away from this example is that God values and honors our faith (beliefs) based on the desire to please Him. Simply: "God said it and I believe it."

Relationships

Another category of God's economy has to do with His desires in our relationships with each other. The book of Proverbs is loaded with wise directions about how to behave toward others and warnings about how not to behave. To illustrate some of this direction, we will go through a number of verses from Romans 12.

Let love be without dissimulations (hypocrisy). Abhor that which is evil; cleave to that which is good. Be kindly affectioned one to another with brotherly love; in honor preferring on another (Romans 12:9-10).

This speaks to a kind loving brotherly attitude that prefers others ahead of you. Such practice will result in a warm, friendly atmosphere that builds trust and respect.

Not slothful in business; fervent in spirit' serving the Lord (Romans 12:11).

This guidance produces a hardworking, high energy, diligent and efficient business person, whether an employee or employer. Their attitude will be positive because they see this activity as serving the Lord. I have read that in the first century, believer slaves brought a premium in the market place because they were hard workers and honest.

Distributing to the necessity of the saints; given to hospitality (Romans 12:13).

I have experienced this both as a receiver and a giver. As I look back over my life I can recall so many examples of when believers have given to my necessity and shown me hospitality. It has been the privilege of my wife and me to have opportunities to give to the needs of fellow saints and to show them hospitality. Acts 20:35 says, *"It is more blessed to give than to receive."* Part of the design of our home was to provide guest rooms so we can show hospitality. It is indeed a blessing to be able to give and be hospitable.

Bless them which persecute you: bless and curse not (Romans 12:14).

This can be a hard one! Our natural tendency upon being persecuted is to want to become defensive and fight back. Earlier I mentioned my mentor Jim Wright. One time when a ministry in which we were both involved was receiving some persecution, this is the advice he gave me about how to respond: "You can choose to defend yourself or you can let the Lord defend you." This happened many years ago, and I do not recall the circumstance related to the persecution; but I do recall that we chose to let the Lord defend us, and the end result was that He did.

Rejoice with them that do rejoice, and weep with them that weep (Romans 12:15).

We are to connect with others based upon where they are in the moment. We can be their cheerleaders or their comforters. Such a spirit builds a sense of community and support. It is good to not be alone whether rejoicing or weeping.

Be of the same mind one toward another. Mind not high things, but condescend to men of low estate. Be not wise in your own conceits (Romans 12:16).

Seek to be in agreement with others. A key factor in doing this is not to think too highly of yourself, particularly thinking you are better than others. Although Americans would like to think we are a classless society, in fact our culture is filled with manufactured standards that produce a sense of rank.

Some of the factors that come into play are financial status, level of education, family of origin, location of your home, and sadly, in some cases ethnic or racial background. This is not to be so for the believer because everyone is a creation of God and loved and valued by God.

> *Recompense to no man evil for evil. Provide things honest in the sight of all men. If it be possible, as much as lieth in you, live peaceably with all men* (Romans 12:17-18).

Don't get caught up in getting even when evil is thrust upon you. For those looking upon you, they should see an openly honest person. We should make every effort to remain at peace with all men. There is a qualifier here because there are interactions with others in which they refuse to be peaceful but, on our part, we are to strive to be the peacemaker and peaceful one.

> *Dearly beloved, avenge not yourselves, but rather give place unto wrath: for it is written, Vengeance is mine, I will repay, saith the Lord* (Romans 12:19).

The temptation to give "pay backs" is strong when we have been wronged. The instruction is to not let our wrath take over because of a very important reason:

> *For the wrath of man worketh not the righteousness of God* (James 4:20).

God is just and He will mete out the vengeance as needed. God has both the complete knowledge of the situation and all the necessary power to do the appropriate vengeance. Since vengeance is His, He will do it when and how He pleases. We can relax and there is no need to get angry because He will take care of it. What a great place to rest!

> *Therefore if thine enemy hunger, feed him; if he thirst, give him to drink; for in so doing thou shalt heap coals of fire on his head. Be not overcome of evil, but overcome evil with good* (Romans 12: 20-21).

In the act of returning good for evil, the evil doer's conscience is exercised. The bigger picture is that God is not willing any should perish, and He is seeking the lost. Depending on the response of the evil doer to your act of kindness and good, this could be the catalyst to bring someone to the Lord.

> *The goodness of God leads thee to repentance* (Romans 2:4).

By not responding to evil, we become players in God's seeking the lost. We are warned to not let the evil overcome us. There is so much evil in the world, including that which is beyond our daily life, that it can become oppressive. Knowing that God is at work in the midst of all the evil will help us not become overcome.

In summary, we see that the scriptures are full of specific instructions that we are to obey and believe. The knowledge of these instructions is what forms the beliefs that will drive our practice. The challenge is to acquire the knowledge and then always to really believe. I am convinced from my own experience that the question I must ask is: "Do I really believe?" Is that also true for you?

Chapter 16

What About Sin?

"Sin has to be cleansed, *sins* must be forgiven; the Redemption of Jesus Christ deals with *sin.*" (Oswald Chambers, *My Utmost for His Highest*).

There have been a number of references to sin so far and several implications about sin, but let's look more closely at sin in reference to our journey toward godliness. Let's start with some clear statements of the definition of sin in the scriptures.

For whatsoever is not of faith is sin (Romans 14:23).

For sin is the transgression of the law (I John 3:4).

Therefore to him that knoweth to do good, and doeth it not, to him it is sin (James 4:17).

Here is the proposition: In their commitment to be godly, believers will seek to know and believe the truth as revealed by God in the scriptures. The truth becomes the focus. Is there a scriptural basis for this focus?

Finally, brethren, whatsoever things are true, whatsoever things are honest, whatsoever things are just, whatsoever things are pure, whatsoever things are lovely, whatsoever things are of good report; if there be any virtue, and if there be any praise, think on these things (Philippians 4:8).

This verse confirms where our focus on our thinking should be. There is nothing in this verse that would suggest that we focus on sin. Then what should we do about awareness of sin?

How do we become aware of sin? Paul said: *"For by the law is the knowledge of sin"* (Romans 3:20). To paraphrase: by knowing the truth and comparing it with what we believe, what we say, what we do, what we think, and finding that there is not a match, then we can identify sin.

Another illustration: To determine if something is level or plumb in construction, we use a tool called a level. If the bubble is not centered, we say that something is not true. The assumption is the measuring tool is accurate. I once constructed a wall and used a level to be sure the wall was plumb. My eye told me that the wall was not plumb, but I went ahead and trusted the level and finished the wall. It still did not look right. Later I used another level and found out my eye was correct. The level I used had been damaged and was not accurate. However, we can be confident that the scriptures are true.

The revelation of sin is also enhanced by the work of the Holy Spirit. The truth revealed is vital to our understanding about what to believe and do and critical to recognizing sin. When we are not believing what we should be doing or not doing what we should, the presence of the Holy Spirit in each believer in a super natural way actively provides revelation.

Jesus said:

> *Howbeit when he, the Spirit of Truth, is come, he will guide you into all truth: for he shall not speak of himself; but whatsoever he shall hear, that shall he speak: and he will show you things to come. He shall glorify me for he shall receive of*

What About Sin?

mine, and shall shew it unto you. All things that the Father hath are mine: therefore said I, that he shall take of mine, and shall shew it unto you (John 16:13-15).

In these three verses, the entire Trinity is involved in showing us the things of God and guiding us into all truth. Now that we have discovered how to identify a sin, what do we do with this knowledge? For sure, we don't want to continue in the sin because a key motive for seeking to become godly is our desire to please the Lord by not sinning.

Besides, the awareness of the sin has brought with it a sense of guilt. The Apostle Paul when lamenting over his awareness of sin cried out:

O wretched man that I am! Who shall deliver me from the body of this death? I thank God through Jesus Christ our Lord (Romans 7:24-25).

There is relief from the burden of guilt through Jesus Christ our Lord. This is wonderful!

But let's look to scripture to be more specific. We find the answer in I John 1:8-9,

If we say that we have no sin, we deceive ourselves, and the truth is not in us. If we confess our sins, he is faithful and just to forgive us our sins, and to cleanse us from all unrighteousness.

Let's face it, we are going to sin. As the verse says, that is the truth. We are sinners.

What to Do

However, the directions are clear and tell us what we are to do upon our awareness of sin and then what God will do in response.

Our part is to confess the sin. That means name the sin. Then God's part is to forgive us and cleanse us. God is faithful and just to forgive us and to cleanse us.

The justice in God's forgiveness is based upon the historical fact that Christ died for our sins and the cleansing is a restorative act. This exercise is an act to restore and maintain relationship. As the Spirit of God guides us into all truth on our journey into godliness, He convicts us of a sin and wants us to pause, confess, and be cleansed so we can continue on down the road of our journey in fellowship with God. This is a terrific provision for us.

We can travel through life thinking on that wonderful list from Philippians and when the awareness of the presence of sin interrupts, we obediently take that confessing, forgiving, cleansing pause, and then continue on our way. You can see that the Lord has thought of everything. Praise the Lord!

The principle of belief drives practices is demonstrated here by first believing in the necessity of confession and then believing in the faithfulness of God in forgiveness and cleansing. The benefiting practice is the relief from guilt and restoration of fellowship with God.

The effect of the continuing walk with the Lord is an increased sensitivity to sin. The awareness of the restorative experience of confession, forgiveness, and cleansing provides encouragement and motivation to acknowledge and address sin as it becomes apparent to us.

Let's pause and look at the concept of relationship in the context of what we are exploring. Sin blocks relationship, particularly close relationships. Stop and think if this hasn't happened to you. I know it has happened to me. You sense something is not right between you and another individual. You may have picked up on some body language or voice tone. This is unsettling, and you explore what is happening. Here are some possible questions that you may ask: Is something the matter? Did I do something to offend you? Did I say something wrong? Did I forget something? Often the answer to the question can lead to a discussion that will result in reconciliation and restoration of the relationship. This is the goal.

However, the path may not be easy. If the questions are asked in a defensive matter, it may exacerbate the tension. If the offended party is defensive, that can also be a problem. It may take time for wounded feelings to subside. The point is there was some kind of sin that blocked the relationship.

If restoration is to be achieved, the sin needs to be identified, confessed, and forgiveness granted. We accept this as part of the human condition. A relationship with a holy God can be blocked by sin. The Lord in His mercy through the work of the Holy Spirit working in us creates awareness that there is a block between us and the Lord, and it is sin. Praise the Lord, He has provided a process for removing the block and restoring relationship!

Levels of Sin

Any sin is contrary to holiness and unacceptable to God, however, we tend to differentiate sins in levels. Certainly, there does appear to be levels of sin that are clearly harmful to individuals and others. For example: murder, adultery, stealing, lying, and deceiving are serious, and a person committed to becoming godly would not participate in these kinds of sin. Some sins are visible before others and some are hidden. There are also sins of deeds and sins of thought. There are attitudes that are sinful. However, there are some more subtle sins that we want to address.

Let's look at how this might manifest to a person wishing to please the Lord by becoming more godly. For an example, let's pick kindness from the list of the fruit of the Spirit listed in Galatians five. The presumption is that a believer believes the truth that the Lord is pleased when the believer is kind.

An interaction occurs with another individual, and upon reflection the believer concludes that his response to the other person was not kind. This conclusion would have been stimulated by the Holy Spirit. Since the believer knows that the "good" thing to do would have been to be kind and based on that knowledge the believer was not kind, then this failure in kindness is sin.

We determined this from the definition of sin found in James 4:17, *"Therefore to him that knoweth to do good, and doeth it not, to him it is sin."* The believer, having been sensitive to the Holy Spirit, is now in position to activate the confession, forgiveness, and cleansing application from I John 1:9.

Because of God's faithfulness and justice, restoration of fellowship is achieved. Perhaps the nature of the unkindness would require some restorative act by the believer. Perhaps there would be a need for an apology and asking for forgiveness or simply a do-over, and this time acting kindly. Can you see that we could use many other examples of God's expectations for godly behavior as stated in His Word and follow the same process?

What we have is a pattern of awareness followed by restoration. Most of the time, this experience would not be particularly traumatic and actually would become rather routine. However, sometimes the failure to meet the Lord's revealed expectation might be very dramatic and lead us to serious repentance. This might involve having created hurt in someone else.

It is good to stop and remind ourselves that these desirable qualities of attitude and behavior that we see in scripture are qualities of God. This is so obvious that it seems silly to state it but after all, being godly does mean being like God. When we think about how lovely these attitudes and behaviors are, it makes us appreciate God even more.

Once again let's remind ourselves that the motivation for the believer in seeking to become godly is a desire to please the Lord. That desire is linked with the believer's love for God. The love for God drives the believer to the practice of being godly, and the belief in God's love for the believer stimulates the response of the believer to love God. I John 4:19 says, *"We love him, because he first loved us."*

As we cycle through the process that we have been discussing and it becomes routine in relationship maintenance, we discover that being godly is not so much a matter of doing as it is a matter of being. Being godly becomes who we are. This is what it means to be transformed with a renewed mind. This is the marvel of the mystery of godliness. It is also the goal. As the refining growth process progresses, head knowledge becomes heart knowledge. The progression is toward deeper understanding. Hannah Hurnard captures this idea with the phrase: "Higher up and further in."

What to Discard

Looking a little deeper at the transaction of a renewed mind and the journey to godliness, we see the teaching of the put off/put on process. What does this mean? We have explored the discarding of beliefs based on **not-truth**, which will drive us into practices that are not godly; and we have explored the accepting of beliefs that are based on the **truth**, which will drive us into practices of godliness. Paul gives us instruction that may be helpful in understanding how this part of the mystery of godliness plays out.

> *That ye put off concerning the former conversation the old man, which is corrupt according to the deceitful lust; And be renewed in the spirit of your mind; And that ye put on the new man, which after God is created in righteousness and true holiness* (Ephesians 4:22-24).

> *And above all these things put on charity, which is the bond of perfectness* (Colossians 3:14).

I like the visual of changing clothes. For example, if I have been working outside wearing what I call my "work clothes," and my wife and I have decided to go out to dinner in town, I will change into my "good clothes." Simply "put off" the work clothes and "put on" the good clothes. This is a straightforward transaction.

Practically, the way it works with our belief drives practice principle is: I put off the **not-truth** belief and put on the **truth** belief. Now the principle can function as designed. Once again, we see the scriptures have provided a model that is helpful in our understanding more about the mystery of godliness.

David's Great Sin

Let's look at a story from the Bible to further explore the nature of sin.

> *And the Lord sent Nathan unto David. And he came unto him, and said unto him, There were two men in one city, the one rich and the other poor. The rich man had exceeding flocks and herds. But the poor man had nothing save one little ewe lamb, which he had bought and nourished up; it grew up together with him, and with his children; it did eat of his own meat, and drank of his own cup, and lay in his bosom, and was unto him as a daughter. And there came a traveler unto the rich man, and he spared to take of his own flock and of*

What About Sin?

> *his own herd, to dress for the wayfaring man that was come unto him, but took the poor man's lamb, and dressed it for the man that was come to him. And David's anger was greatly kindled against the man; and he said to Nathan, As the Lord liveth, the man that hath done this thing shall surely die: And he shall restore the lamb fourfold, because he did this thing, and because he had no pity. And Nathan said to David, Thou art the man. Thus saith the Lord God of Israel, I anointed thee king over Israel, and I delivered thee out of the hand of Saul; And I gave thee thy master's house, and thy master's wives into thy bosom, and gave thee the house of Israel and of Judah and if that had been too little, I would moreover have given thee such and such things. Wherefore hast thou despised the commandment of the Lord, to do evil in his sight? thou has killed Uriah the Hittite with the sword, and has taken his wife to be thy wife, and has slain him with the sword of Ammon* (II Samuel 12:1- 9).

The Holy Spirit drills sins down to their root in the process of renewing our minds and transforming believers into the image of Christ. I suspect that each sin under careful examination would reveal that in some way the sin is connected either to not loving God wholeheartedly or not loving our neighbor as our self.

The story of David and Bathsheba is an illustration of the drilling down. God uses Nathan to confront King David about this awful and embarrassing sin. Obviously, both the sin of adultery and murder are clearly visible. King David had broken two of the Ten Commandments. He must have known this.

However, King David's sin was deeper than that. It also seems clear that the sin of lust led to adultery, and in light of Bathsheba's pregnancy, the sin of seeking to cover the sin led to murder. King David named his sin in response to Nathan's story. King David's sin was lack of pity. The story of the rich man taking the poor man's only ewe lamb in spite of having many sheep of his own revealed an abuse of power. The power differential between the rich man and poor man was clearly illustrated. The issue of power differential between King David and Bathsheba and Uriah was also at play.

The weaker could only resist the stronger at their peril. In the book of Daniel there are two stories—the lions' den and the fiery furnace—that demonstrate the risk of defiance of the weaker against the stronger. The stories are famous because God intervened and rescued. The influence of power differential is recognized in our government's laws concerning crimes perpetrated by a person in authority.

I like to think of pity more in terms of mercy. Here is one definition of pity: sympathetic or kindly sorrow evoked by the suffering, distress, or misfortune of another, often leading one to give relief or aid or to show mercy.

Too often we think of a pitiful person as someone who is lacking and deficient. Mercy speaks of showing kindness and being gentle. It speaks of not taking advantage of another. Often as part of my feedback to teachers in the courses I teach, I have reminded them of the power differential that they possess over their students and encourage them to be gentle.

It is my belief that the only appropriate time to use a power differential is when a person has the responsibility of rendering judgment or discipline, and then it often can be done with some tenderness and gentleness and still be effective.

King David's failure to show pity or mercy was a failure in love.

He failed in demonstrating his love for God and failed in showing love for his neighbor. Drilling down to the root of King David's sin revealed his heart. I contend that the Holy Spirit, as He reveals the root sins to believers, is drilling down to the basic attitudes that need to be changed into godly attitudes. A variety of sins may manifest because they are driven by the root sin. King David's root sin of not having pity or showing mercy manifested as adultery and murder.

Attitude

It has been my experience that this drilling down to a root attitude is true for me. I am thinking in the area of the root sin of selfishness. A common malady for most of us, my selfish attitude can be manifested in many ways. Another root sin that I often contend with in my journey to godliness is laziness. Don't get me wrong, I am not a lazy person in the way we generally think of laziness. However, I know that two of my personal strengths that have served me well are the strengths of being a maximizer and being a strategic person. These strengths have served me well in my quest for efficiency and effectiveness.

But I get a nagging feeling, which I believe is from the Holy Spirit, that sometimes my motivation for efficiency and effectiveness may have something to do with being lazy and finding an easy way. I confess this lingering challenge because I believe it may very well be a drilling down into my heart and motives by the Holy Spirit. Hmmmm!

When we look for the application of belief drives practice to this situation, a question comes to mind. What is the truth belief that should exist to avoid the sin of not showing pity as covered in the above example? I believe that the attitude of empathy is what is to be believed to prevent the failure to show pity.

Let's explore! Had King David had empathy toward Bathsheba, he would have considered the tremendous pressure that he could apply because of his position as king. He would have realized how hard it would have been for Bathsheba to resist or rebuke him for his inappropriate and sinful behavior. Had King David had empathy toward Uriah, he would have considered that a loyal soldier would without question feel obligated to obey his king and return home from the battle as ordered. Uriah was such a man of honor and character who had empathy toward the men under his command that he refused to sleep with his wife because his men were unable to return home to their wives. Uriah's character spoiled King David's plan to divert his responsibility for Bathsheba's pregnancy.

Although not mentioned in the story, King David also did not show empathy for Uriah's commander, Joab, because he ordered him to place Uriah in a dangerous position in the battle so that Uriah would be killed. Joab was under pressure to obey the King no matter what, even if it made him indirectly an accomplice in the death of Uriah.

Let's think about this and look for a personal application regarding empathy. Like it or not, every culture and society has systems of rank. We clearly see very specific systems of rank in the military and law enforcement. We also see rank in governments and businesses.

Often the ranking systems are accompanied with titles. I have had several titles in my life: teacher, principal, director, superintendent, professor, doctor, dad, grandfather, and eldest son. I have also held offices: president of an organization, treasurer, captain of a team. These titles were associated with an area of responsibility and rank. With many of these titles, I had a status as to proper protocol

What About Sin?

in how I was addressed: Mr. Daniel or Dr. Daniel. We know the phrase, "Rank has its privileges." I must admit that with each of these titles, I felt like I had a lot more responsibility than privileges.

However, there is status with rank. Rank can come simply because a person is bigger or older. The background truth is that rank doesn't matter to God. God is not a respecter of persons. Apparently, there was a problem with people not showing empathy in the early church. James addresses this:

> *My brethren, have not the faith of our Lord Jesus Christ, the Lord of glory, with respect of persons. For if there come unto your assembly a man with a gold ring, in goodly apparel, and there come in also a poor man in vile raiment: And ye have respect to him that weareth the gay clothing, and say unto him, Sit thou here in a good place; and say to the poor, Stand thou there, or sit here under my footstool: Are ye not then partial in yourselves, and are become judges of evil thoughts? Hearken my beloved brethren, Hath not God chosen the poor of this world rich in faith, and heirs of the kingdom which he hath promised to them that love him? But ye have despised the poor. Do not rich men oppress you, and draw you before the judgment seats? Do they not blaspheme that worthy name by which ye are called? If ye fulfill the royal law according to the scriptures, Thou shalt love thy neighbor as thyself, ye do well. If you have respect to persons, ye commit sin, and are convinced of the law as transgressors* (James 2: 1-9).

We don't want to leave this discussion without acknowledging that those of lower rank are already intimidated by those of higher rank. This makes them vulnerable to being oppressed and even more important for those of higher rank to show pity and be gentle to those of lesser rank. Since we are not to show specialized respect to individuals as demonstrated in the scripture, and God has clearly declared that it is a sin, we ought to be loving.

> *Let nothing be done through strife or vainglory; but in lowliness of mind let each esteem others better than themselves. Look not every man also on the things of others. Let this mind be in you, which was also in Christ Jesus: Who, being in the form of God, thought it not robbery to be equal with God: But made himself of no reputation and took upon him the form of a servant, and was made in the likeness of men: And being found in fashion as a man, humbled himself, and became obedient unto death, even the death of the cross* (Philippians 2:3-8).

God outranks us all! He is Father, Lord, Master, Teacher, Savior, Creator. God shows us empathy. He knows we are as dust. He is gentle, caring, kind, and patient. Aren't you glad that our heavenly Father is empathetic toward us?

The Issue Is Not the Issue

Before we leave this story and discussion, let's look at another construct that is illustrated in this story. The construct is: the issue is not the issue. What does this mean? I first became aware of this construct while practicing talk therapy. Here is how it was applied. During talk therapy, through probing questions, while the counselee speaks about the concerns that brought them to counseling, the counselor is also working on the theory that the presented issue may not be the real issue.

Often the real issue that needs to be addressed is hidden from the counselee. Perhaps if the real issue was recognized, there would not have been a need for counseling because the counselee may have been able to resolve the issue on their own. However, the problem needed a new set of eyes. The presented issue hides the truth. The truth is necessary for resolution.

What About Sin?

When we bring this concept into our construct, belief drives practice, it becomes clear that the real issue is what needs to be believed in order to drive the practice to the desired thinking and/or behavior. Also, we can see that recognizing the real issue is essential to gaining understanding in our quest for discovering Who am I? and How does the world work? However, through the years, I have learned that this construct—the issue is not the issue—has many applications.

Now let's apply this construct to the story of David's great sin. As we have mentioned, the apparent presenting issue was the very serious sins of adultery and murder. However, Nathan's story revealed that the real issue was lack of pity as demonstrated with David's abuse of the power differential.

It is interesting that the Lord had Nathan use a story to reveal to David his real sin issue rather than having Nathan just confront David with his lack of pity. By using the story, Nathan was able to show rather than tell. I suspect that the insights we gain into the real issues in our life may come from stories or illustrations that show us the real issue rather than a direct telling. Can you see that this is another example of the mystery of godliness?

As we recognize that the Holy Spirit is working in each of us by drilling down to get to issues of the heart, we can see that He is out to reveal the real issue. Before we continue, let's pause and discuss the difference between acts of sin and attitudes of sin. David's story clearly illustrates this. Adultery and murder were acts of sin, but the lack of pity was an attitude of sin. We can also acknowledge that the lust that led to the adultery was also an attitude of sin. Can we think of some other examples?

Jesus said,

> But I say unto you, that whosoever looketh upon a woman to lust after her has hath committed adultery with her already in his heart (Matthew 5:28).

The Heart

Let's try to grasp the importance of the issues of the heart by looking at a positive example. Isn't each item listed in the fruit of the Spirit issues of the heart? Is not each one of them an attitude? Think of it—love, joy, peace, patience, kindness, goodness—all are attitudes and issues of the heart. In the journey to godliness we are looking at a transformation where the **not-truth** of sinful attitudes are replaced by the **truth** of positive godly attitudes in our belief system. These are heart issues.

The loving way the Spirit of God draws us into a godly relationship with the Lord is very touching and precious when we think about it! He patiently guides us past our fears and concern about imagined costs for following and obeying the Lord. It is a refining process to move through the journey to godliness.

Chapter 17

Journey to Godliness

The journey of a thousand miles begins with one step (Lao Tzu).

All journeys have secret destinations that of which the traveler is unaware (Martin Buber).

Have faith in your journey. Everything had to happen exactly as it did to get you where you are going next (Mandy Hale).

Not everyone will understand your journey. That's fine. It's not their journey to make sense of. It's yours (Lessons from Life).

Although we have implied that the path to godliness is a journey, we have not really explored the journey. I found many clever and poignant quotes about a journey. Not only is it a journey, but it is a personal journey. There are many variables involved because we are unique individuals.

Each one of us has a unique body—so unique that we can be specifically identified by finger prints or DNA. Our bodies vary in size, shape, and specific characteristics. There are variations in strength and health. We vary in birth order and family of origin size. There are variations in IQ and giftedness, both natural and spiritual. There are variations in location: where we were born, were raised, and the places where we have lived. We vary in family dynamics and values experiences. We also vary in extent and quality of educational experiences. We have had unique opportunities, secrets, disappointments, and traumas.

Jerry Bridges in his book, *The Practice of Godliness*, observes:
> The author of Hebrews likens it to a distance race which must be run with perseverance. Our Christian experience is not a sprint that is soon over; it is a distance race that lasts a lifetime. It requires perseverance, because the reward—the object of our hope—is in the distant future" (p. 216).

For believers, there is the mysterious working of the Holy Spirit along the journey. We have longings, convictions, promptings, warnings, inspirations, and enlightenment. All of these variations make up our unique personality. In *My Utmost for His Highest*, Oswald Chambers develops the concept of personality for the believer:

> Personality is that peculiar, incalculable thing that is meant when we speak of ourselves as distinct from everyone else. Our personality is always too big to grasp. An island in the sea may be the top of a great mountain. Personality is like an island, we know nothing about the great depths underneath, consequently we cannot estimate ourselves. We begin by thinking that we can, but we come to realize that there is only one Being Who understands us, and that is our Creator.

> Personality is the characteristic of the spiritual man as individuality is the characteristic of the natural man. Our Lord can never be defined in terms of individuality and independence, but only in terms of personality, "I and My Father are one." Personality merges, and you only reach your real identity when you are merged with another person. When love, or the Spirit of God strikes a man, he is transformed, he no longer insists upon his separate individuality. Our Lord never

spoke in terms of individuality, of a man's "elbows" or his isolated position, but in terms of personality—-"that they may be one, even as We are one." If you give up your right to yourself to God, the real true nature of your personality answers to God straight away. Jesus Christ emancipates the personality, and the individuality is transfigured; the transfiguring element is love, personal devotion to Jesus. Love is the outpouring of one personality in fellowship with another personality (p. 347).

Can you sense the mystery in this quotation? Paul said, in Philippians 1:21, *"For me to live is Christ."* Here we have a marvelous transformation: the wonder of a changed life because a believer becomes a changed person. We have to admit that this is miraculous! It is evidence of *"beyond"* and *"other."* Grasping this concept makes many verses in scripture make sense.

To whom God would make known what is the riches of the glory of this mystery among the Gentiles; which is Christ in you, the hope of glory (Colossians 1:27).

Not Alone

Scripture supports the individuality and uniqueness of believers in the body of Christ (the church). The Apostle Paul states in 1 Corinthians 12:

(v. 1) "Now concerning spiritual gifts, brethren I would not have you ignorant."

(v. 4) "Now there are diversities of gifts, but the same Spirit."

(v. 5) "And there are differences of administrations, but the same Lord."

(v. 6) "And there are diversities of operations, but it is the same God which worketh all."

(v. 7) "But the manifestations of the Spirit is given to every man to profit withal."

(v. 8) "For to one is given by the Spirit the word of wisdom; to another the word of knowledge by the same Spirit."
(v. 9) "To another faith by the same Spirit; to another the gifts of healing by the same Spirit."
(v. 10) "To another the working of miracles; to another prophecy; to another discerning spirits; to another divers kinds of tongues; to another interpretation of tongues;"
(v. 11) "But all these worketh that one and the sameself Spirit by dividing to every man severally as he will."
(v. 12) "For as the body is one, and hath many members, and all the members of that one body, being many, are one body: so also is Christ."
(v. 14) "For the body is not one member but many."

Clearly these verses show diversity of gifts given to believers, but also it is important to note that the gifts are for the *profit* of all, and the gifts are distributed as the Lord wills (verse 11). In Ephesians 4:11-13 Paul proclaims:

> *And he gave some, apostles; and some, prophets; and some, evangelists; and some pastors and teachers; For the perfecting of the saints, for the work of ministry, for the edifying of the body of Christ: Till we all come in the unity of faith, and of the knowledge of the Son of God, unto a perfect man, unto the measure of the stature of the fullness of Christ.*

We can see an element of the mystery of godliness revealed in the way the Spirit is working through the distribution of spiritual gifts to individual believers in the body of Christ. The purpose of the spiritual gifts is to build up the saints in ways that result in personal growth and leads to unity and a community of love. We can see that the mystery of godliness is very complex and we have yet to explore further some of the opposition that believers face in the journey to becoming godly.

Need to Know

Part of the mystery of godliness has to do with the unique journey that each believer takes. There are many variables that influence our path to godliness. A big variable has to do with each individual's knowledge of the truth. We are talking about knowledge of the truth as revealed by God in the scriptures.

It sounds silly to say, but the following is very accurate: "You don't know what you don't know." We are talking about ignorance, and the cure for ignorance is knowledge. It seems obvious that the more truth you know, the more truth you can choose to believe. The principle of belief drives practice works more efficiently in achieving godliness if there is more truth available for the person to believe that will drive the result of their godly practice.

A related variable has to do with intensity and diligence in seeking to learn more from the scriptures, hearing Bible teachers, and reading sound authors of biblical truths. These also contribute to increased knowledge and are a provision from the Lord. Associations in a Bible believing fellowship of believers is also very useful.

Closely associated is a healthy curiosity for wanting to understand: Who am I? How do I work? How does the world work? from God's perspective. This curiosity drives a person to seek understanding with diligence, trying to figure it all out. Two verses come to mind:

> *It is the glory of God to conceal a thing: but the honour of kings to search out a matter* (Proverbs 25:2).

> *But without faith it is impossible to please him: for he that cometh to God must believe that he is, and that he is the rewarder of them that diligently seek him* (Hebrews 11:6).

It seems that God is saving His precious truths for those who are really committed to learning them. The summary of this variable is the quantity of knowledge of truth that a believer knows and believes will have a direct influence on the journey to godliness. In addition, the intensity of commitment to increasing this knowledge driven by a desire to please the Lord and understand His ways also will have an influence on it.

Another related variable has to do with an attitude by the believer to seek the guidance of the Holy Spirit. Although knowledge of the scripture provides significant guidance, the direct activity of the Holy Spirit in the daily life of the believer is an influence on the path to godliness. The believer needs to be aggressively praying and asking for guidance and be in tune with the direction provided directly from the Holy Spirit. This involves hearing the voice of God in our heart, which may seem sort of mystical because it is clearly in the *"beyond"* and *"other"* arena.

Looking at the variables around, we see our unique individuality. We each have unique personalities and temperaments, talents and giftedness, including spiritual gifts. We also have unique bodies and health issues. The Lord created us and knows us much better than we know ourselves. He has plans for us.

> *For we are his workmanship, created in Christ Jesus unto good works, which God hath before ordained that we should walk in them* (Ephesians 2:10).

These unique differences all fit into the journey of each individual's mystery of godliness.

Circumstances

Everyone's life has a unique set of circumstances and experiences. The Lord works in these circumstances to move us in the direction of becoming more godly. First of all, since the Lord already knows everything He is not surprised when stuff happens to us. We can state the obvious; we see some circumstances as good and some as bad. Let's pause and look at couple of verses.

And we know that all things work together for good to them that love God, to them who are the called according to his purpose (Romans 8:28).

My brethren, count it all joy when ye fall into divers temptations; Knowing this, that the trying of your faith worketh patience. But let patience have her perfect work, that ye be perfect and entire, wanting nothing (James 1:2-4).

When the circumstance seems good, we shout, "Oh yes!" When the circumstance seems bad we shout, "Oh no!" The unique opportunities, disappointments, and losses are part of the circumstances. The influence of circumstances around each person's vocation and avocation all shape who we are. The Lord works in these circumstances to influence our opportunity to look to Him for understanding on how this relates to our journey to godliness. Remember each circumstance is an opportunity to choose a truth to believe as it relates to our relationship to God.

Beginning and End

Let's pause and consider this characteristic of a journey. It is assumed that each journey has a beginning and an end. But each journey also has a "daily," which implies that the journey has a yesterday and a tomorrow. All have value and relevance, but our journey is experienced in the daily, the now, the present. Each daily has its own circumstances.

The Lord's grace for the daily circumstance is provided in that moment when we need it. We don't need grace for yesterday because it is past, and we don't need grace for tomorrow because it hasn't happened. Yet, how often do we fret about yesterday and tomorrow, seeking grace for what is over and for what may not even happen.

Let us therefore come boldly unto the throne of grace, that we may obtain mercy, and find grace to help in time of need (Hebrews 4:16).

Therefore do not worry about tomorrow, for tomorrow will worry about itself. Sufficient to the day is its own trouble (Matthew 6:34).

Everyone will have many people enter into their life. We will develop close relationships with some people and others will only be acquaintances. These people may be people that are colleagues at work, a spouse, relatives, or neighbors. Many other people we will only observe and will never have any relationship with them. The point is that each individual has their own unique montage of people in the circumstance arena. In a mysterious way, all these encounters work to influence our journey to godliness.

The unique feature of each family of origin is another variable. Our families of origin play a major part in the shaping of what occurs in our transformation and renewing of our minds. In our families, we may have been nurtured or abused. These experiences can impact how we tend to see ourselves and how we see God. There will be aspects of the family of origin that will assist our journey to godliness and others will need to be overcome in our journey.

Where we live is another variable and this can really vary. In this category of variable, we can include where we were raised, all the different places we may have lived, and where we are presently living. Each community has unique characteristics that include its weather, the community culture, the ethnicity make up of the citizens, and even more closely, the neighbors and friends that we knew and presently know.

Some people spend their entire life in one location; however, more commonly people live in many different locations and in many different homes. Each location will have its influence on our experiences and circumstances that will shape our journey.

Awareness

Although there are probably other variables that influence our journey, I have saved this particular variable to discuss last. The sequence of awareness of sin is an interesting variable. Remember that the Holy Spirit makes us aware of sin either through the scriptures or a troubling of our conscience. Either way, there is a mysteriousness about the experience.

It is an awareness of the **truth** and its application that gives us the awareness of sin because sin is aligned with a **not-truth**. We need the transaction of replacing the **not-truth** with the **truth** in our belief systems so the **truth** will drive us to the practice of godliness.

The Lord in His sovereign will and specific love orders the sequence in which we become aware of a specific sin that is blocking our progress in our journey to godliness. The order of revelation of sin is unique to each individual and consistent with the Lord's divine purpose for each one.

In light of the variables we have been discussing, I like to think of the individual journey as a composition for an orchestra. There are many different performers on many different instruments playing many different notes. The conductor directs all the various parts together to produce the music. Each part is important and each note and each instrument is to be played in the proper order to achieve the desired sound—beautiful music.

Each musician along with the conductor must make the proper decision of what to play and when to play it to achieve the desired sound. In a precise way the proper note at the proper time represents the truth, and the musician must believe that it is the truth so that their decision will drive the practice, which is the desired sound.

I can envision the Lord being the conductor for each believer's life and directing each variable to play its proper part at the proper time in composing each person's beautiful journey into godliness.

I am burdened to expound even more about the journey of the mystery of godliness even risking blatantly expanding on the obvious. For every one of us, our journey is uniquely our own. It is personal and private. Probably most of the journey is so private that only we know about it. This is the kind of private that is also secret.

This private secret is about who we are, where we have been, and where we are going. My journey is my journey—the good, the bad, the fun, the exciting, the embarrassing, the boring, the lonely, and the special. You can say the same thing about your journey as can everyone who has ever lived, is living, and will live. Just think about that!

Long Journey

Our journeys are spread out on a continuum. There is an old saying, "a thousand-mile journey begins with one step." All of our journeys have a beginning, and we progress day by day. Each of these journeys are made of stories. Actually, we could think of our journeys as a chain of stories. Think about how often we reveal or share part of our journey in the form of a story. The stories are sections or segments chained together to make up our overall journey.

I meet monthly for coffee for about an hour with some retired guys that my wife calls my cronies. There are five of us. I worked with three of them, and all of us worked professionally as administrators in education. What do we talk about? It varies, but mostly it involves stories either about current events or activities from the past. I enjoy it very much. My dad had his set of stories as well. My father-in-law lived with my wife and me the last seven years of his life, and he told us many stories.

My grandfather was a great story teller, and all the grandchildren loved his stories. I remember many of them and have repeated them often. There is a story about how as an eleven-year-old, he spent the summer painting the wire on a woven wire fence for a sugar factory in northern Colorado. He was paid a small amount each day. Then there was the story about how he lost an eye when he was a kid after being hit in the eye by a baseball. I loved to sit by him in church (he would slip me some candy), and he would ask me not to sit on his blind side.

One of my favorite Grandpa Jones stories had to do with an experience he had related to his teaching a boys' Sunday School class. He had assigned the boys the task of coming up with a slogan for the class to be reported the following Sunday. To no surprise to my Grandpa Jones, no one came to class with a slogan but he was prepared with one, "Keep your mind on what you are doing while you're doing it."

Decades later while Grandpa was visiting his brother at his house, one of the boys that had been in his class, now of course an adult with children who was a professional electrician, was working in the basement. Grandpa bent down at a basement window and called out, "What are you doing?" The instant reply was, "Keeping my mind on what I'm doing while I'm doing it." Some take-aways from this story: First, it is good advice for staying focused on thought or deed. Second, it speaks to how a person's influence can last for many years.

All these stories are precious memories and continue to be passed along to others. Each story was a segment from their journey. The news reports we hear on the radio, read in the newspaper, or see on television are stories. Sometimes personal experience stories are shared about the witnessing of an accident or a crime or the loss of a friend or pet.

My wife and I have a shared a journey with a whole assortment of experiences. We have gone through the loss of all four of our parents as well as the loss of other relatives and friends. We have gone through job changes and moving to different locations as well as building a house. The journey has been full of adventures, fun trips, great visits with relatives and friends, and a few surgeries. Within this shared journey, there are many story segments. The shared journey is a blessing, but within the shared journey we each have our own personal private journey with our own stories.

You can probably think of many different shared journeys you have experienced, but the bottom line that we repeatedly come back to is the reality that we each one of us have our very own unique, private, personal, secret journey filled with segmented stories.

Although we have been talking about shared stories from our journeys, I suspect that we all have many stories that we have not shared. We could have many reasons for not sharing them. Perhaps we don't think they are relevant to anyone else or the stories are too mundane and unimportant. Perhaps the stories are embarrassing or just too personal. It is possible that most of our stories are never shared.

By now, I am sure you are wondering where I am going with all of this and how does it relate to our journey to godliness. Here is the punch line. Although I have been emphasizing that we are alone on our personal, private, secret journey, that is not really the whole story. We are not alone. The Lord has been with us all along. He was there in the past, will be there in the future, and is with us now. Follow the logic!

Among the attributes of God there is omniscience and omnipresence. God knows everything and is everywhere and always has been. Based on this truth, He has always been with us. He has been with us when we were alone and in tears during a dark night. He was there when we have been hurt. He was there during times of great joy and glee. He was there when we received bad news. He is not only there but He is involved. We are not alone. This is a mystery.

However, there is more. The Lord knows all about those secret, private and personal stories and experiences. We have experienced surprises from the unexpected, but the Lord was not surprised. Since the Lord knows all, He knew what was going to happen in our journey. What happened was not unexpected by the Lord.

It's All Good

The mystery of godliness intensifies because we have established that when a person comes to Christ, the Holy Spirit indwells the believer. The indwelling of the Holy Spirit is part of the package for the children of God. Brace yourself and look at this verse:

> *We know that all things work together for the good of those who love God: those who are called according to His purpose* (Romans 8:28).

All things! Could this possibly be true? Mysteriously all those events and stories in the journey of each person who loves God work together for good. Somehow all of these things play a role in becoming godly. This is really *"other"* and *"beyond"*! Mostly, I suspect we will not figure out how this all works, but it must be true because this truth is clearly declared in scripture.

Let me share a personal story from my journey that I have never shared before. It is one of those personal, private, and secret stories. It is a story of a failing on my part. It may shed some light in how all things, even failures can work together for good.

When I was in my early teens and after I had come to the Lord, an incident occurred on the playground. Some classmate, and I don't remember if it was a boy or girl, made a comment in response to some event or activity. Again I don't remember what it was about, but here is what my classmate said to and about me: "Oh, he is religious!" I suspect that the classmate probably knew that my family went to church regularly.

My failure was when I simply replied, "Oh no, I'm not!" To me this was more than denying being religious, it was denying the Lord Jesus and my relationship with Him. I could identify with Peter. The rooster didn't crow, but I sensed the message. I have confessed and I am confident that the Lord has forgiven and cleansed me, but the memory of that story is vivid in my mind. I have determined that I never want to deny the Lord Jesus ever again. By God's grace, I don't think I have; and by His grace, I never will.

This bad deed was part of "the all things" that has worked together to build this resolve. I am guessing that you can join me in looking back down the long chain of stories in your journey to godliness and identify and recognize many of the all things that have worked together for your good. We cannot move forward without looking at this verse as we walk through our journey to godliness.

For we are his workmanship, created in Christ Jesus unto good works, which God hath before ordained that we should walk in them (Ephesians 2:10).

In the Rear-View Mirror

In reflection, each of us can look back on the path we have been traveling in our transformational journey of a renewed mind to become godly. As a senior citizen, I can look back on the way the Lord has brought me and recognize a role all these variables have played on my journey. I would not presume to think that I can recognize all the variables or the role they played because I know there is mystery present that involves the *"other"* and the *"beyond."*

As I look backward at the trail I have traveled made up of stories and variables, I see events, circumstances that defy an explanation but clearly were an act of God. I am sure you may have heard the saying, "It was a God thing." or "God's fingerprints are all over this." This is the mystery of godliness. As you join me in contemplating the way the Lord has led, think about these verses.

I will remember the works of the Lord: surely I will remember thy wonders of old (Psalm 77:11).

This I recall to my mind, therefore have I hope. It is of the Lord's mercies that we are not consumed, because his compassions fail not. They are new every morning: great is thy faithfulness. The Lord is my portion, saith my soul; therefore will I hope in him (Lamentations 3:21-24).

And thou shalt remember all the way which the Lord thy God led thee these forty years in the wilderness, to humble thee, and to prove thee, to know what was in thine heart, whether thou wouldest keep his commandments, or no (Deuteronomy 8:2).

Andrae Crouch said it all so well in his hymn, "Through It All" when he wrote that everything he's experienced, through it all he's learned to trust in Jesus and thank Him for all of it.

Chapter 18

What About Relationship?

> Thank God for every one who has learned that the dearest friend on earth is a mere shadow compared with Jesus Christ. There must be a dominant, personal, passionate devotion to Him, and only then are all other relationships right (Oswald Chambers, *My Utmost for His Highest*).

Before moving into the issues around opposition to godliness, let's pause and look more closely at the matter of relationship. Throughout our exploration there has been an implication of relationship, and we certainly have seen it in our recent look at individuality, personality, and gifting in the church. It has been established that we are created in the image of God.

God is relational as revealed in the mystery of the trinity, Father, Son, and Holy Spirit. Scripture tells that they are One. They are in complete harmony, totally aware of each other and what each is doing. Although scripture at times indicates specific functions of each, sometimes the functions overlap. It is very logical that a relational God would seek a relationship with His creation.

Let's start with our creation. We have established that the created is the property of the Creator and that the Creator has discretion about the makeup and design of His creation (Potter and clay). Since we are God's creation, we start our existence with the relationship of Creator and created. Our creation began in the mind of God.

His attributes of all knowing and having always known mean that each one of us is the product of a specific decision and action of God. Since God is relational, He wants a relationship with each person of His creation. Since God is also holy, sin created a barrier to having a relationship. God's love for His creation moved Him to find a solution to removing the barrier. His solution was a very costly one, the sacrificial death of the Lord Jesus. Oh, how He loves us!

After the necessary work of reconciliation on God's part, it becomes necessary for the individual person to do their part by accepting the redeeming work of the Lord Jesus. We have already discussed at length how this can happen and how a part of the salvation experience includes the indwelling of the Holy Spirit. When an individual becomes a believer, the capacity for a relationship with God has been established and the journey toward godliness is underway.

Let's spend a little time exploring the implications of what it means to be relational. For most of us, our relational experiences begin in our birth family and particularly our mother where the relationship began in the womb. Initially, it has a lot to do with survival. The mother provides the essentials for survival.

When you stop to think about it, many future relationships will be in some way connected to survival. Family relationships develop with all the plusses and minuses that can occur. Relationships develop with extended family and neighbors followed by relationships created in school. So it goes through the life journey.

What About Relationship?

As a senior citizen, I can reflect back over many years and many relationships. Some of the relationships were very close for a while but have since ended mostly because of changes in locations and circumstances. Some relationships have ended because of differences and conflicts. Some relationships have endured through the years and are highly valued. There is my wonderful relationship enjoyed on a daily basis with my dear wife. Some relationships are casual and can best be categorized as simply acquaintances.

Some relationships have been particularly helpful during a crisis period in life. Other relationships are mostly related to business or professional activities. As a career educator, I have had relationships with multiple students, teachers, and parents. Most of them have been pleasant but others not so much. I am sure that I must have had thousands of relationships with people.

Relationships have something to do with our heart because there is some level of caring involved that is usually somewhat mutual, although we are likely mostly aware of the caring on our part. In the advancing of my years I have observed that my caring level has gone up. I suspect that it has something to do with my transformation in my personal mystery of godliness journey. If I am right, imagine how much God cares for us!

There is also sadness about lost or ended relationships that leads to a sense of lamenting. Now, I am mostly retired but I still teach some university courses online. I have noticed that through the process of reading students' assignments and giving feedback, a sense of relationship develops.

In many of the courses, we begin with a brief introduction from each other and then progress on through the course. I find that I experience a sense of sadness and lamenting after the course is over.

This relationship is with people that I never meet in person and probably will never meet, and don't even know what they look like.

Yet, I still have a feeling of loss at the end of the course. One student who took several courses with me was particularly verbose and shared information about his family and freely shared his opinion on the challenges and problems in education. I even invited him to come for a visit if he was ever in our area. I find that since his last course, I miss him. All of this reflection indicates to me how important relationships are in my life.

Let's explore a little further. Just think about relationships that develop between people and their pets and other animals. Think about the lavish demonstrations of affection that people show their pets and often the pets reciprocate. We name our pets and often spend great amounts of money on them. We grieve when they pass away. While we are on the subject of animals, just think about how relational many animals are with each other.

Although the relationships may be important to survival, there still appears to be some indications of affection and connectedness. Many prey animals, both domestic and wild, are gregarious. They stick together in herds and become anxious and agitated when separated. The relationships between mother animals and their babies are often very intense. We delight in watching them, and many nature programs are built around stories of mother-baby relationships.

Our relational God has built relationships into His creation. His desire to have a deep and intense relationship with His children only makes sense in the realm of "how things work." His pursuit of a relationship with His children also makes sense in the realm of "who we are" and who He is.

What About Relationship?

It is exciting to think about how deep and rich the potential relationship with God can be and how deep and rich that relationship is promised to be for God's children for eternity. God does not lack in relationship capacity, and because the Holy Spirit dwells in us, we do not lack in relationship capacity. Also, because we have been created as relational beings, we have a hunger and thirst for deeper relationship. Not only is this a clue about the mystery of godliness but it is also the goal.

Chapter 19

Who Are the Enemies?

> The great triad of enemies for Christian growth contain the world, the flesh, and the devil (R. C. Sproul).

It is good to remind ourselves that the principle we have been following all along—belief drives practice—is complex. It may sound simple and mechanical, but there are many variables and contingencies involved. We understand that the belief needs to be based on truth in order to result in a godly practice. In review, we remember the many variables that are involved because of unique individuality and our unique experiences on our personal journey.

To add to this complexity, the scripture clearly teaches that believers have three enemies who are committed to opposing believers on their path to godliness: the world, the flesh, and the devil. We will identify and define each one, but the good news is we find in scripture instructions and tools for contending with them as we move ahead in our path of transformation. Before we go on in this topic, let's be reassured by scripture.

> *Now the Lord is that Spirit: and where the Spirit of the Lord is, there is liberty. But we all, with open face beholding as in a glass the glory of the Lord, are changed into the same image from glory to glory, even as by the Spirit of the Lord* (2 Cor. 3:17-18).

Who Are the Enemies?

The World

When the world is identified as an enemy of believers, the world in this sense is a system of activities, attitudes, and values that are opposed to God and His kingdom. The world operates from the realm of "**not-truth**." The world's purpose is to draw people away from God and then become committed to the world's program. We sometimes speak of worldliness. To further our understanding let's look at references to the world system from scripture.

Ye adulterers and adulteresses, know ye not that friendship of the world is enmity with God? Whosoever therefore will be a friend of the world is the enemy of God (James 4:4).

Love not the world, neither the things that are in the world. If any man love the world, the love of the Father is not in him. For all that is in the world, the lust of the flesh, the lust of the eyes, and the pride of life, is not of the Father, but is of the world. And the world passeth away, and the lust thereof: but he that doeth the will of God abideth forever (I John 2:15-17).

And we know that we are of God, and the whole world lieth in wickedness (I John 5:19).

For the grace of God that bringeth salvation that appeared unto all men. Teaching us that, denying ungodliness and worldly lusts, we should live soberly, righteously, and godly, in the present world (Titus 2:11-12).

Grace be to you and peace from God the Father, and from our Lord Jesus Christ, Who gave himself for our sins, that He might deliver us from this present evil world, according to the will of God and our Father. To whom be glory for ever and ever. Amen (Galatians 1:3-5).

The world system excludes God. The parts of the world system that are vile and corrupt are often easy to identify. There are parts of the world system that are more subtle and harder to recognize. A good test question when trying to discern if an activity or attitude is worldly is: "Where is God in all of this?"

The challenge is often to recognize how not to be of the world while still being in the world. For the present, believers are destined to exist in this present evil world as they move through their own mystery of godliness experience in route to a renewed mind and a godly lifestyle.

Another question for discernment is: "Am I operating my life as if God were not involved?" The challenge in answering this question comes because believers may be only excluding God in part of their life and operating on worldly values in that part. This error can contaminate the belief in the truth by accepting a "**not-truth**."

Another error that can occur is that in an effort to not be conformed to the world, believers will set up a set of laws of outward behavior to be considered righteous. This can become a merit-based mentality in which favor with God is perceived to be acquired. The good news is as we struggle with discerning that which is worldly and therefore enmity with God, the Holy Spirit is working to clarify and reveal that which displeases the Lord.

The Flesh

The flesh is another enemy. This is serious!

> *Because the carnal mind is enmity against God: for it is not subject to the law of God, neither indeed can be. So then they that are in the flesh cannot please God* (Romans 8:7-8).

What do we mean by the flesh? Biblical commentaries explain the term "flesh" with the words like: self, sin nature, old nature, old man, or fallen nature. One of the effects of the fall of man has been

Who Are the Enemies?

that ever since Adam, everyone has a tendency to seek to operate their lives independently from God. Generally, the awareness of this inward struggle only manifests itself as a believer seeks to live a godly life. We will look more closely at what Paul describes in the struggle with the flesh in Romans 7.

What shall we say then? Is the law sin? God forbid. Nay, I had not known sin, but by the law: for I had not known lust, except the law said, Thou shall not covet. But sin, taking occasion by the commandment, wrought in me all manner of concupiscence. For without the law sin was dead. For I was alive without the law once: when the commandment came, sin revived, and I died. And the commandment, which was ordained to life, I found to be unto death. For sin taking occasion by the commandment, deceived me, and by it slew me. Wherefore the law is holy, and the commandment holy, and just and good. Was then that which is good made death unto me? God forbid. But sin, that it might appear sin, working death in me by that which is good; that sin by the commandment might become exceeding sinful.

For we know that the law is spiritual: but I am carnal, sold under sin. For that which I do I allow not: for what I would, that do I not; but what I hate, that do I. If then I do that which I would not, I consent unto the law that it is good. Now then it is no more I that do it, but the sin that dwelleth in me. For I know that in me (that is, in my flesh,) dwelleth no good thing: for to will is present with me; but now to perform that which is good I find not. For the good that I would I do not: but the evil which I would not, that I do. Now if I do that I would not, it is no more I that do it, but sin that dwelleth in me. I find that then a law, that, when I would do good, evil is present with me. For I delight in the law of god after the inward man: But I see another law in my members, warring against the law of my mind, and bringing me into captivity to the law of sin which is in my members.

O wretched man that I am! Who shall deliver me from the body of this death? I thank God through Jesus Christ our Lord. So then with the mind I myself serve the law of God; but with the flesh the law of sin (Romans 7:7-25).

This passage is not easy to understand because the struggle is confusing in the mind of believers. Paul is explaining how he discovered that although he wanted to obey the law and do right and please God, there was something operating within him that was resisting this desire. He establishes that the law is the good and the appropriate standard and by the statements of the law comes the knowledge of what God's expectation is.

Yet, when he seeks to do right, then sin is working in his mind. The solution Paul proclaims is that Jesus Christ our Lord can deliver us. There is a way out of the dilemma of the struggle with the flesh, and it is found in submission to the Lord and a change in thinking with a renewed mind. The path to godliness comes back to believing and practicing the truth.

Clearly, there is a struggle! There are two takeaways we want to grasp. The first is there is an internal war going on in the mind of each believer between the new nature of the Holy Spirit indwelt believer and the old nature of being a sinner in the image of Adam. The second is the glorious provision that there is victory and freedom through Jesus Christ the Lord.

Believers have a capacity to live free from dominance of the old nature and rest in the new nature. Since it is a war, there are many battles. As Paul points out, it is the knowledge of truth (the law) that reveals the old nature and the desire to do right that reveals the struggle to do right. In practical application in the journey to godliness, the struggle will continue in a progression. It is the knowledge of the truth and the commitment to believe the truth that will lead to a step-by-step movement to godliness.

It is important that believers acknowledge this truth and embrace it. Sadly, this truth is often not taught to believers, nor do they discover it in their own study. When this truth is not integrated into the believer's life, they remain what the scripture calls carnal i.e. operating in the flesh. They believe effort to please God can come from their own efforts and be seen as having merit rather than the result of resting and abiding in Christ. Can you see how an alliance with a worldly point of view and the old nature can multiply the enemy's impact on believers?

What does this struggle look like on a daily basis? The struggle could be around our ability to actually believe the truth that has come into our life and awakens the resistance from the old nature. It is important to recognize that the old nature is sin and contrary to God. Now that I realize this fact, what do I do? We find the answer in I John 1:9,

If we confess our sins, He is faithful and just to forgive us our sins, and to cleanse us from all unrighteousness.

Our part is to confess our sins. The Lord's part is to forgive and cleanse. He is faithful and just because all of our sins have been paid for on the cross, and the cleansing erases the sense of guilt.

Failure to believe that our sins are forgiven and that we are cleansed can leave a person carrying a burden of guilt. This guilt is actually another sin. Remember that forgiveness gives freedom and peace. In reality, this process is ongoing because the Spirit of God will faithfully convict of sin. The confession and cleansing will move us to a commitment to not continue in sin. The new belief will drive our practice to a godly behavior that is pleasing to God.

At this point when we look at the weight of this struggle, we need a little more comfort.

> *My little children, these things write I unto you, that ye sin not. And if any man sin, we have an advocate with the Father, Jesus Christ the righteous: And He is the propitiation for our sins: and not for ours only, but also for the sins of the whole world* (I John 2:1-2).

The Devil

The third enemy is the devil or Satan. The whole sin thing began in a rebellion in heaven before the creation when Satan rebelled against God and was cast out of heaven. Scripture is clear that Satan is actively involved in a war against God and His Kingdom. In some ways you could think of mankind as collateral damage.

We can indulge ourselves in wondering why the God who can control everything has allowed this war to happen but to do so is to begin to question God. Remember there is the factor of *"other"* and *"beyond."* In the book of Revelation, we see that ultimately God will triumph, and Satan will be defeated and vanquished.

It is critical that we as believers accept the reality that Satan is actively opposing God in the world and that includes Satan personally opposing each one of us in our individual lives. Let's look at some scriptures that expose some of Satan's current activity in the world.

> *Be sober, be vigilant; because your adversary the devil, as a roaring lion, walketh about, seeking whom he may devour. Whom resist stedfast in the faith, knowing that the same afflictions are accomplished in your brethren in the world* (I Peter 5:8-9).

Who Are the Enemies?

And that they may recover themselves out of the snare of the devil, who are taken captive by him at his will (II Timothy 2:26).

And no marvel; for Satan himself is transformed into an angel of light (2 Corinthians 11:14).

He that committeth sin is of the devil, for the devil sinneth from the beginning. For this purpose, the Son of God was manifested, that he might destroy the works of the devil (I John 3:8).

But Peter said, Ananias, why hath Satan filled thine heart to lie to the Holy Ghost, and to keep back part of the price of the land? (Acts 5:3)

Submit yourself therefore to God. Resist the devil, and he will flee from you (James 4:7).

Put on the whole armour of God, that ye may be able to stand against the wiles of the devil (Ephesians 6:11).

Neither give place to the devil (Ephesians 4:27).

And the devil that deceived them was cast into the lake of fire and brimstone, where the beast and the false prophet are, and shall be tormented day and night for ever and ever (Revelation 20:10).

As we peruse the scriptures, we can deduce that Satan is actively seeking to deceive, destroy, influence, ensnare, and induce people to lie and sin. He can transform himself into an angel of light and can appear harmless.

We can also see how we are to respond: resist, stand against the wiles of the devil, and not give place to the devil. We are assured that I John 4:4 , *"greater is He that is in you, than he that is in the world."* If we resist steadfast in the faith, Satan will flee. We are to watch and be vigilant because Satan is our adversary. We are to put on the whole armor of God. We are to recover ourselves out of the snare of the devil. Ultimately, we see Satan cast into the lake of fire to be punished with torment for ever and ever.

Jerry Bridges in his book, *The Practice of Godliness,* describes a misconception that occurs in the life of believers:

> One of the many ways in which the devil tries to devour us is related to the meaning of his name. The Greek word for devil means "accuser," or "slanderer." As the prince of slanderers, he accuses man before God, but he also slanders God to man. One of the thoughts that often enters our minds when we are undergoing trials is, "If God really loved me he would not have allowed this to happen to me." Or, "If God loved me, he would provide a way out of this trying situation." Such thoughts come from the devil; failure to recognize this origin causes two problems. First, we assume those thoughts originate within our own hearts, so we add a sense of guilt for thinking harsh thoughts about God to our already anxious mind. Now we have both anxiety and guilt to contend with, compounding our problem. Second, we fight the wrong battle. Instead of resisting the devil, we try to deal with our own wicked hearts. Although there are plenty of times when we do have to deal with our own wicked hearts, this is not one of them: this is a time to resist the devil. We have a clear command, coupled with a promise. "Resist the devil, and he will flee from you" (James 4:7) (p. 195).

We see that the three enemies of believers—the world, the flesh and the devil—are opposing and resisting our efforts to become godly. In addition, both recognizing and understanding that this resistance exists is valuable information for understanding both how the world works and who I am.

Who Are the Enemies?

If it were not for the wonderful assurance that God is in us, for us, and with us, the battle would be totally depressing. The assurance that believers are the Lord's and He has enabled us with His life by the indwelling Holy Spirit, plus He has given us guidance through His word gives us confidence to commit to the journey to godliness.

Chapter 20

Cause and Effect

Every why hath a wherefore (William Shakespeare).

Now let's examine how this plays out on a daily basis in our lives. The principle of cause and effect operates in how the world works and in some ways in discovering who we are. Actually, our principle of belief drives practice operates on the cause and effect principle. The belief is the cause that activates the drive to produce the practice, which is the effect. Everyone operates on this principle many times each day.

When we see an effect (result), we look for the cause. We have words we use in the search for the cause: explore, investigate, research, diagnose, inquire, assess, and search, for example. If the effect that occurred is desirable, we search for the cause so we can repeat the cause to ensure continued desirable results. However, if the effect is undesirable, we search for the cause to discover what is to be avoided to remove the undesirable result.

Operating with the cause and effect principle begins early in life. For example, a newborn baby cries and the baby's mother hears the crying. The mother assumes that there is a cause for the baby crying. The crying of a baby is not desirable. The mother goes to the baby to seek to determine what is causing the crying.

Cause and Effect

The baby may be hungry, may need to be changed, may be too cold or too hot, may have a tummy ache and need to be burped, or may have been frightened. Whatever the cause, the mother will seek to eliminate it. When the cause has been addressed, the baby will stop crying and all is well. Now the baby soon learns that if the baby will cry (cause), the effect will be for the baby's mother to come to the rescue and fix the problem. The cause and effect principle works for both the baby and the mother.

This simple illustration is useful but when you think about it, our lives are permeated with the cause and effect principle. As I type and view the screen, I note that my pressing on a key (cause) produces the appearance of a letter (effect) on the monitor. Perhaps it would be helpful to think of the concept of one-to-one correspondence. Essentially one cause produces one effect. One push on a keyboard key produces one letter to appear.

Let's explore a little deeper. How to go about discovering causes? Generally, we use our physical senses: sight (eyes), hearing (ears), smell (nose), taste (mouth) and sense of touch. Our bodies are wonderfully made with a system of nerve endings that work as sensors.

Messages are sent to our brains where they are processed, and the whole brain system discussed earlier does the processing. With these inputs we are prepared to respond to addressing the cause. You are probably thinking that this really makes sense and is very obvious. Please tell me something I don't know or haven't thought about before.

What if the cause is invisible and not detected by our physical senses? There can be emotional causes that we sort of feel in our bodies and are aware of them, but it is hard to identify which of the five physical senses are in play. What about fear? What about joy? What about pleasure? What about sadness? These could all definitely be causes that have results. Some results that we see as good and others we see as bad.

Looking closer at an example of an invisible cause, pause and think of the wind. We cannot see the wind even though we can sometimes feel it on our skin, but we can see the effects of it. Knowing about the wind as a cause is important in so many ways. Pilots need to know about the wind's speed and direction. Instruments have been developed to measure both the speed and direction of the wind. People in sailboats are concerned about the wind as are firemen. Weather forecasters include wind speed and direction in their forecasts. Interestingly, the Spirit of God is compared to the wind in scriptures.

Which leads me to a critical point. There are mysterious invisible causes that originate with God that are active in our world and in our individual lives. Also, there are mysterious invisible causes that originate in the world—the flesh and the devil that are active in our world and our individual lives. It is critical in the development of our belief system that we acknowledge these invisible forces are active in our lives and influencing our journey to godliness.

The closer we look at our transformation and renewing of our minds as believers, the more we see how complex, comprehensive, and involved the process is. We also can see that without the enabling of God, the journey is impossible. This speaks to our need to be completely dependent on God and to be assured that the Lord is able to bring it to pass.

We can also rest in the assurance that it is the will of God to create this change in each one of us. Ultimately, each believer will be changed to the extent that each will become a spotless bride of Christ. It is good to keep in mind that what we are seeing and experiencing here is not all that there is. There is more to come, and it will be wonderful for those that are in Christ Jesus.

Chapter 21

Desire to Seek

"Now we need to understand that what simply *occupies* our mind very largely governs what we do. It sets the emotional tone out of which our actions flow, and it projects the possible course of action available to us." (*Divine Conspiracy*, Dallas Willard, p. 324).

Love

And now after all of this, why do we desire to seek godliness? What is the motivation for becoming godly? In a word: love! Stop and think of it. It makes sense. We are created in the image of God and God is love. The importance of love is repeatedly proclaimed in scripture. Let's look at some scriptures and notice the preeminence and the expansiveness of love:

> *For God so **loved** the world, that he gave his only begotten Son, that whosoever believeth should not perish, but have everlasting life* (John 3:16).

> *Behold what manner of **love** the Father hath bestowed upon us, that we should be called the sons of God* (I John 3:1).

> *Beloved, if God so **loved** us, we ought also to **love** one another. No man has seen God at any time. If we **love** one another, God dwelleth in us, and his **love** is perfected in us.*

Desire to Seek

*Hereby know we that we dwell in him, and he in us, because he hath given us of his Spirit. And we have seen and do testify that the Father sent the Son to be the Savior of the world. Whosoever shall confess that Jesus is the Son of God dwelleth in him, and he in God. And we have known and believed the **love** that God hath to us. God is **love**; and he that dwelleth in love dwelleth in God, and God in him. Herein is our **love** perfect, that we may have boldness in the day of judgment: because as he is so are we in this world. There is no fear in **love**; but perfect love casteth out fear: because fear hath torment. He that feareth is not made perfect in **love**. We **love** him, because he first **loved** us. If a man say, I **love** God, and hateth his brother, he is a liar: for he that loveth not his brother whom he hath seen, how can he **love** God whom he hath not seen? And this commandment have we from him, That he who **loveth** God **love** his brother also. Whosoever believeth that Jesus is the Christ is born of God: and everyone that **loveth** him that begat **loveth** him also that is begotten of him. By this we know that we **love** the children of God, when we **love** God, and keep his commandments. For this is **love** of God, that we keep his commandments: and his commandments are not grievous* (I John 4:11-21—I John 5:1-3).

*And now I beseech thee, lady, not as though I wrote a new commandment unto thee, but that which we had from the beginning, that we **love** one another. And this is **love**, that we walk after his commandments, That, as ye have heard from the beginning, ye should walk in them* (II John 5-6).

*Whom having not seen, ye **love**; in whom, though now ye see him not, yet believing, ye rejoice with joy unspeakable and full of glory: Receiving the end of your faith, even the salvation of your souls* (I Peter 1:8-9).

*Owe no man any thing, but to **love** one another, for that **loveth** another hath fulfilled the law* (Romans 13:8).

*This is my commandment, That ye **love** one another, as I have **loved** you. Greater **love** hath no man than this, a man lay down his life for his friends. Ye are my friends, if ye do whatsoever I command you* (John 15:12-14).

*These things I command you, that ye **love** one another* (John 15:1).

*Ye have heard that it hath been said, Thou shalt **love** thy neighbor, and hate thine enemy. But I say unto you, **Love** your enemies, bless them that curse you, do good to them that hate you, and pray for them which despitefully use you* (Matthew 5:43-44).

*The Lord appeared of old unto me, saying, Yea, I have **loved** thee with an everlasting **love**; therefore with **loving**kindness have I drawn thee* (Jeremiah 31:3).

*A friend **loveth** at all times, and a brother is born for adversity* (Proverbs 17:17).

*But God, who is rich in mercy, for his great **love** wherewith he **loved** us, Even when we were dead in sins, hath quickened us together with Christ, (by grace ye are saved* (Ephesians 2:4-5).

*And to know the **love** of Christ, which passeth knowledge, that ye might be filled with all the fullness of God* (Ephesians 3:19).

*With all lowliness and meekness, with longsuffering, forbearing one another in **love**; Endeavoring to keep the unity of the Spirit in the bond of peace* (Ephesians 4:2-3).

Desire to Seek

*But speaking the truth in **love**, may grow up into him in all things, which is the head, even Christ* (Ephesians 4:15).

*He brought me to his banqueting house, and his banner over me is **love*** (Song of Solomon 2:4).

*Thou shalt **love** the Lord thy God with all thy heart, and with all thy soul, and with all thy strength, and with all thy mind, and thy neighbor as thyself* (Luke 10:27).

These verses (including my emphasis) are just a sampling of the declarations and descriptions of love in the scriptures. First Corinthians 13 is an entire chapter dedicated to the importance of love. In the kingdom of God, love is the motivation for all activity. Love gives and love cares. The love of God gives us the capacity to care in a way that grows as we progress on our journey to godliness.

Notice how the sense of caring expands beyond people and issues that are near us even to strangers in faraway lands. Our loving God is a caring God. He cared so much for and about us that the Lord Jesus came to earth to be a sacrifice for our sins. Isn't God's love amazing? The desire to choose to seek godliness is driven by love that is placed in the believer by God! Love is the answer for the way things work in the kingdom, and love is the answer for who I am. We are loved and we are made to be one who loves. Love wants to know Jesus and love wants to obey Him. I Peter 2:7 says, *"Unto you therefore which believe he is precious..."*

Jerry Bridges in his book, *The Practice of Godliness*, describes love giving:

> In I John 3:16 John says, *"This is how we know what love is: Jesus Christ laid down his life for us."* The key idea here is that *love gives, even at great cost to itself.* Jesus gave his life for us. John 3:16 tells us that the Father so loved that he gave

his only Son for us. In Jesus' incarnation and death, both the Father and the Son gave in response to our desperate plight. Nothing but the Savior's incarnation and death would suffice to rescue us. The cost was infinite, but God the Father and God the Son loved us so much they did not hesitate to pay the cost to meet our need (p. 249).

I came to know the Lord when I was twelve years old. I can't say that I remember anything else specific about my twelfth year, but I do remember my decision for Christ. My parents were believers and we attended a Bible believing church. Most of my close friends are believers. I spent most of my professional life working in believer ministries. I have been surrounded by likeminded people who also love the Lord Jesus.

I can remember the stunning conclusion I reached while attending a secular university and the discussion moved into areas of "religion." There were classmates who actually hated the Lord Jesus. I remember how it hurt me to hear them talk that way because to me He is precious. The journey to godliness is for those who know and love the Lord Jesus. Simon Peter said, in John 6:68-69,

Then Simon Peter answered him, Lord, to whom shall we go? Thou hast the words of eternal life. And we believe that thou art the Christ, the Son of the living God.

For the believer there is no other choice but a commitment to make the journey to godliness, knowing that a renewed mind will be transformed. It is a delightful thought!

Being confident of this very thing, that he which hath begun a good work in you will perform it until the day of Jesus Christ (Philippians 1:6).

Epilogue

For me the epilogue is an opportunity for reflections. I reflect on: What was my goal? What was my purpose? Was I clear? Did I accomplish my goal? Did I address my audience? You may have noticed that I asked a lot of questions in this writing. Sometimes the questions were used as an introduction, and I proceeded to attempt to answer them. Other times the questions went unanswered. This is mystery.

You may ask: What was the intended audience? It is good practice for speakers, teachers, or writers to have a vision of their intended audience. My intended audience was you. I envision you as a believer who sincerely loves the Lord and is committed to living a life that is pleasing to Him.

You are seeking to learn more about Him and how to demonstrate your love for Him through obedience to His Word. You believe that the Bible is the word of God and is your source of truth. I also believe that if this were not so, you would probably have never started the book and would not likely be reading the epilogue.

My goal is that after reading this book, you would have an increased sense of how much the Lord loves you and how you are valuable and precious to Him. We tend to assess value by cost. Think about what it cost the Lord to save you from your sins so you could become a child of God. In addition, think about the investment the Lord has made by providing you a Comforter and guide with the indwelling of the Holy Spirit. And if that was not enough, He is preparing a place for you. Indeed, you are very precious and valuable to the Lord.

The Mystery of Godliness

Your journey toward godliness is a destination. Your journey is a good thing. You are not alone on your journey because all God's children are on their journey. Hopefully you are experiencing a sense of burden lifted. Much about your life has not and is not necessarily easy, but since the Lord is working in you the way is easier. It is not all up to you. That should make you smile. Your journey to godliness will yield the fruit of the Spirit. That is a beautiful thing.

The path to godliness is still the mystery of godliness. Mysteries are a good thing. I hope you see that. This particular mystery has promises within it. It is good for now and good for your future. It is nice just to meditate on it. Here is a challenge: As you read your Bible, notice the words: godliness and godly. Also in contrast, notice what is said about the ungodly. Be sure to notice the word, truth, particularly in the epistles.

In searching for a "big picture" summary that would capture the essence of a renewed mind and a life transformed resulting from the mystery of godliness, I found such a summary in Dallas Willard's *Divine Conspiracy*. I think it was part of his summary of his book. I repeat it here because it seems so appropriate for a view of the journey to godliness.

> What, then, should we expect to happen as we move onward in the eternity where we live even now? Let us break it down into three stages: the time of growing steadily, the time of passage, and the time of reigning with Jesus.
>
> THE TIME OF GROWING STEADILY. We should, first of all, find ourselves constantly growing in our readiness and ability to draw direction, strength, and overall tone of life from the everlasting kingdom, from our personal interactions with the Trinitarian personality who is God. This will mean,

Epilogue

most importantly, the transformation of our heart and character into the family likeness, increasingly becoming like "children of the Father, the one in the heavens" (Matt 5:45)

The *agape* love of I Corinthians 13 will increasingly become simply a matter of who we are. But the effects of our prayers, words, and deeds—and sometimes of our mere presence—will also increasingly be of a nature and extent that cannot be explained in human terms. Increasingly what we do and say is "in the name of the Lord Jesus Christ" and every part of our life becomes increasingly eternal...We are now co-laborers with God. (page 396)

When with a godly imagination you gaze upon the Lord Jesus and admire Him, don't you want to be like Him? I do!I close with the lines from an old hymn, *More About Jesus*.

> More about Jesus would I know,
> More of His grace to others show;
> More of His saving fulness see,
> More of His love who died for me.
>
> More about Jesus let me learn,
> More of His holy will discern;
> Spirit of God, my teacher be,
> Showing the things of Christ to me.
>
> More about Jesus; in His word,
> Holding communion with my Lord;
> Hearing His voice in every line,
> Making each faithful saying mine.
>
> More about Jesus on His throne,
> Riches in glory all His own;
> More of His kingdom's sure increase;
> More of His coming Prince of Peace.

References

A-Z Quotes. http://www.azquotes.com/

Bridges, J. (1983). *The Practice of Godliness*, Navpress, Colorado Springs, CO.

Chambers, O. (1935). *My Utmost for His Highest*, Barbour and Company, Inc, Westwood, NJ.

Eldredge, J. & S. (2005). *Captivating,* Thomas Nelson, Inc., Nashville, TN.

Packer, J. I. (1973). *Knowing God,* InterVarsity Press, Downers Grove, IL.

Peterson, E. (2005). *Christ Plays in Ten Thousand Places*, Wm. B. Eerdmans Publishing Co., Grand Rapids, MI.

Tozer, A. W. (1961). *Knowledge of the Holy*, Harper and Row, Publishers Incorporated, New York, NY.

Verploegh, H. (ed.) (1987). *Oswald Chambers: The Best from All His Books,* Oliver Nelson Books, Cambridge, Ontario.

Willard, D. (1998). *Divine Conspiracy,* HarperCollins Publishers, New York, NY.

Willard, D. (2012). *Hearing God*, Intervarsity Press, Grover, IL.

About the Author

Dr. Elden Daniel lives in the San Luis Valley, located in south central Colorado. He and his wife are empty nesters and live on a 160-acre farm where Elden grew up. In 2007, they moved into a new house built on the site of the old farm house where he lived as a boy. They have two horses, some sheep, two birds, and three cats. Elden enjoys fishing for trout in the irrigation reservoir located only a quarter of a mile from their house. In addition, Elden likes big game hunting with some of their sons and grandsons each fall. Elden and his wife, Karen, enjoy visits from their children, grandchildren, and friends.

Dr. Daniel is a professional educator with a BA in Elementary Education, an MA in Mental Health Counseling, and an Ed.D. in Educational Leadership. He has been a classroom teacher and school administrator. He served at Colorado Springs Christian School for twenty-two years and in public education as a classroom teacher and as an administrator for fifteen years. He has taught as an affiliate professor for several universities for the last sixteen years, and he is still teaching for two universities. For four years he served as Executive Director of Family Life Services, a Christian ministry. He retired from full time work in 2010. Since then, he and his wife, Karen, are enjoying a quiet life and fellowship with Christian friends and family.

Dr. Daniel is the author and narrator of the audiobook, *Be Ye Thankful* (2020). This audiobook is an exploration into the importance and value of being thankful.

Dr. Daniel is the author and narrator of the audiobook, *What Was She Thinking Series* (2020). This audiobook is a series of short essays about a mother who aborted her baby and is designed to encourage and support those who have chosen the pro-life position.

Dr. Daniel is the author and narrator of the audiobooks, *Adventures in Biblical Thinking Series* (2020). Each volume contains short thinking adventures to stimulate biblical thinking and, in addition, there are a few exercises at the end of each thinking adventure to challenge deeper thinking. This series could be used for small group Bible studies.

Dr. Daniel has a website: https://adventuresinbiblicalthinking.home.blog/ where he posts short articles about adventure in biblical thinking. Please feel free to subscribe.

www.ingramcontent.com/pod-product-compliance
Lightning Source LLC
Chambersburg PA
CBHW072007110526
44592CB00012B/1227